Health Information Management Compliance

A Model Program for Healthcare Organizations

2002 Edition

Sue Prophet, RHIA, CCS

AMERICAN HEALTH INFORMATION
MANAGEMENT ASSOCIATION®

before a criminal or civil investigation began. A compliance program will be effective in preventing and detecting regulatory violations when it has been reasonably designed, implemented, and enforced to do so. Moreover, an effective HIM compliance program is essential to the success of a corporate compliance program because the cornerstone of health information management—documentation of the provision of healthcare services— is the cornerstone of fraud investigations and the evidence of compliance. (See appendix A for a description of HIM background and skills.)

HIM compliance program effectiveness is measured by the success of the outcome (that is, compliance), not by the impressiveness of the processes that have been created. Additionally, the size and scope of a compliance program are not necessarily indicators of its effectiveness. An important objective is to *keep it simple.* Most organizations already have many elements of a compliance program in place. Existing policies, procedures, and standards (policies and procedures pertaining to coding, documentation practices, and health record completion requirements) need to be brought under the umbrella of the compliance program.

Each organization has an affirmative duty to ensure the accuracy of the claims it submits for reimbursement. A sound compliance program requires that reasonable measures be instituted to detect errors and potential fraud in the claims preparation process. Thus, there must be evidence of compliance through detecting, correcting, and preventing coding and billing problems and documentation deficiencies. It is important to note that providers are not subject to criminal, civil, or administrative penalties for innocent errors or negligence. The civil False Claims Act covers only offenses that are committed with actual knowledge of the falsity of the claim, reckless disregard, or deliberate ignorance of the falsity of the claim. The Civil Monetary Penalties Law has the same standard of proof. For criminal penalties, a criminal intent to defraud must be proved beyond a reasonable doubt. While not fraud, innocent billing errors are a significant drain on our health care reimbursement systems. Therefore, providers, Medicare contractors, government agencies, and consumers need to work cooperatively to reduce the overall error rate.

It is not enough to simply develop a compliance program. In addition to being effective, the program must have the full commitment of the organization's governing body, management, and employees. Adherence must be demonstrated at all levels of the organization. The Office of Inspector General (OIG) in the Department of Health and Human Services has indicated that it will consider a poor compliance program, or lack of adherence to the program, as being worse than having no program at all. Compliance controls need to be integrated into the very fabric of the healthcare organization's operations. A compliance program is never finished; rather, it is an ongoing, evolving process for continuous quality improvement.

Benefits of an HIM Compliance Program

The benefits of an HIM compliance program include:

- Development of effective internal controls to ensure compliance with federal regulations, payment policies, and official coding rules/guidelines

- Identification of problematic coding and documentation practices and initiation of prompt and appropriate corrective action

- Improved health record documentation

- Improved education for organizational staff and physicians

- Improved coding accuracy

- Reduction in denials of claims

- Increased productivity due to better communication, more comprehensive policies/procedures, and more efficient operations

- Improved financial performance due to increased productivity and operational efficiency

- Improved collaboration and cooperation among healthcare practitioners and those processing and using health information

- Improved employee performance and morale

- Provision of a mechanism for identifying and reporting unethical HIM practices

- Reduced exposure to civil and criminal penalties and sanctions in the event of a fraud investigation, and if wrongdoing is discovered by the government, a reduction in the severity of imposed penalties

Elements of an HIM Compliance Program

An effective HIM compliance program consists of the following nine elements:

1. Mission
2. Code of conduct
3. Oversight
4. Policies and procedures
5. Training and education
6. Communication
7. Auditing and monitoring
8. Enforcement
9. Problem solution and corrective action

Mission

An HIM mission statement should be formulated that is consistent with the healthcare organization's mission statement. Although its exact wording should be individualized for each organization, just as each healthcare organization's mission statement is slightly different, certain key points should be addressed, including the following:

- HIM staff are committed to ethical and legal business practices.

- HIM staff are committed to making every effort to comply with federal and state statutes and regulations, private payer policies, official coding rules and guidelines, and the accepted standards governing the practice of health information management, including appropriate clinical documentation practices.

- HIM professionals are committed to developing internal policies and procedures that are consistent with reimbursement regulations and policies and official coding rules and guidelines and prohibit coding practices that inappropriately maximize reimbursement.*

- HIM professionals value health information of the highest quality, as evidenced by its integrity, accuracy, consistency, reliability, and validity.

- HIM professionals demonstrate behavior that reflects integrity, supports objectivity, and fosters trust in professional activities.

- HIM professionals refuse to participate in illegal or unethical acts and to conceal the illegal, incompetent, or unethical acts of others.

- HIM professionals believe that collaboration and cooperation among healthcare practitioners and those processing and using health information are essential to ensure high-quality health information and accurate claims submission.

- HIM professionals respect the confidentiality of individually identifiable health information.

Code of Conduct

Along with an HIM mission statement, the healthcare organization should develop an HIM code of conduct. AHIMA recommends that its *Standards of Ethical Coding* be used as the basis for the organization's HIM code of conduct (see appendix E.) Every employee, in addition to contracted consultants and independent contractors (such as outsourced coding staff), involved in the coding function should be asked, initially at the time of employment and annually thereafter, to sign and date a statement affixed to a copy of the code of conduct (see figure 1). The signed copy of the code of conduct should be kept in the employee's personnel file.

An organization may also choose to specifically include adherence to federal and state regulations, payer reimbursement policies, and the organization's own policies/procedures in the code of conduct. The code of conduct should be reviewed annually, perhaps at the time of the annual performance evaluation.

Oversight

AHIMA recommends that an HIM professional with demonstrated honesty and integrity and a strong background in coding be charged with responsibility for overseeing the HIM compliance program. Depending on the size of the organization, this responsibility may be the individual's sole duty or added to other responsibilities. This position is referred to as HIM compliance specialist throughout this document for illustration purposes. However, the specific title of this position may vary from organization to organization.

---

*While maximization of reimbursement is inappropriate and should be prohibited in the organization's mission statement, code of conduct, and policies and procedures—as maximization involves manipulation of the sequence of codes or adding codes that are not substantiated by the health record documentation—optimization is appropriate. Optimization involves sequencing and selecting the codes such that the organization receives the optimal reimbursement to which it is entitled, while adhering to all of the applicable rules and guidelines pertaining to proper coding and documentation.

Figure 1. **Example of a statement regarding the code of conduct**

I have read and understand these *Standards of Ethical Coding* and agree to abide by them at all times. If at any time I believe I have reason to suspect that one of these standards has been violated, either by an internal or external entity, I will report this incident according to the organization's internal reporting policy.

_____   _____
Employee Signature   Date

Depending on the organization's size and structure, this position might either be part of the HIM department or external to the HIM department. Locating this position outside the HIM department allows more objectivity in the responsibilities of this position because the individual will not report to the HIM director, thereby avoiding any potential conflicts of interest. It might make the most sense for the HIM compliance specialist to report to the corporate compliance officer. However, in smaller organizations it may not be feasible for this position to be outside of the HIM department. In any case, this individual should be accountable to the corporate compliance officer and should sit on the organization's compliance committee.

For multihospital systems or integrated delivery networks, one individual should oversee HIM compliance systemwide and one individual should oversee compliance activities at each healthcare organization within the system. The corporate individual should work closely with his or her counterparts at the individual organizations to ensure a consistent, cohesive process for implementation of, and adherence to, the corporate compliance program. Depending on the size of the organization, the person responsible for oversight of the HIM compliance program may or may not have individuals reporting to him or her.

Both the individual responsible for oversight of the HIM compliance program and the HIM director should serve on the organization's compliance committee or task force. An organization may choose to establish a coding compliance committee that is separate from (but reports to), or is a subcommittee of, the corporate compliance committee. The coding compliance committee should include representatives from pertinent departments such as registration, billing, utilization management, and quality management, as well as coding professionals and physicians. This committee should monitor the effectiveness of the coding compliance program, oversee development of policies and procedures related to coding, review results of auditing and monitoring of coding practices, assist with development of audit protocols, and develop educational programs on coding and documentation issues. (Appendix C contains a sample job description for the position of HIM compliance specialist.)

Policies and Procedures

Clear written policies and procedures that are communicated to all employees are important to ensure the effectiveness of a compliance program. Written standards and procedures reduce the prospect of erroneous claims and fraudulent activity by identifying risk areas and establishing tighter internal controls, while also helping to identify any aberrant billing patterns. Comprehensive policies and procedures on coding, documentation requirements (including retention), payer regulations and policies, and contractual arrangements for coding consulting and outsourcing services should be developed. In addition to the statutes, regulations, and guidelines of federal and state health insurance programs, the policies and requirements of private health plans and managed care organizations should be addressed.

All HIM policies and procedures should be approved according to the organization's policy on review and approval of departmental policies and procedures. An up-to-date, user-friendly index for the HIM policies/procedures should be maintained so that specific information can be readily located. In addition, policies and procedures should be kept in a location that is easily accessible to all HIM staff.

In addition to the organization's own policies/procedures, the HIM department should maintain up-to-date resources related to pertinent government regulations and payer policies, including:

- Medicare Manuals

- Other pertinent manuals addressing government requirements such as those dealing with the Minimum Data Set (MDS) and Outcome and Assessment Information Set (OASIS) completion and submission for long-term care facilities and home health agencies, respectively

- Medicare contractor and private payer newsletters and bulletins

- Local medical review policies (LMRPs)

(Key coding references are addressed in more detail under the upcoming section titled Internal Coding Practices, see page 9.) Additionally, AHIMA publications on coding and professional practice standards are excellent resources. Bookmarking useful Web sites in an Internet browser also enlarges one's number of references. The organization's HIM compliance program document should specify where information regarding regulatory or payer-specific requirements can be located.

Risk Assessment

Written policies and procedures should take into consideration the regulatory exposure for each function or department. Organizations should conduct an assessment of the particular risk areas to which they are vulnerable in order to identify potential problems, develop policies/procedures to address them, and prioritize focus areas for educational programs and auditing/monitoring activities. Assessing the level of risk with respect to nationally-recognized high-risk areas is a good place to start. Nationally-recognized high-risk areas include those identified by the following:

- The OIG in its annual work plans, inspection reports, fraud alerts, compliance program guidances, and semiannual reports

- The Centers for Medicare and Medicaid Services (CMS) in its transmittals and program memoranda

- Private payers in their memoranda

- Healthcare experts in journals, newsletters, and other publications

See appendix B for a list of high-risk areas related to HIM that have been identified by the OIG and healthcare experts. Although this list of risk areas is not exhaustive or all-encompassing, it serves as a good starting point for an internal review of the organization's potential vulnerabilities. Areas of risk that are unique to one's organization should also be assessed, through auditing and monitoring (see page 44 for the section titled Auditing and Monitoring), interviews of staff, review of claims denials and rejections, and a review of systems and processes. Identified areas of risk should be incorporated into the organization's policies/procedures, training and educational programs, and auditing/monitoring activities.

HIM policies and procedures should explicitly address weak areas identified through a risk assessment so as to demonstrate that appropriate measures have been implemented to resolve problems or improve system weaknesses. (See page 61 for the section titled Problem Resolution and Corrective Action.) For example, a clinic may discover that a certain procedure is being reported incorrectly because separate codes are being assigned for its individual components (that is, the procedure has been unbundled). A hospital might discover that certain diagnoses are being reported as complications or comorbidities with unusually high frequency. Perhaps there is a high accuracy rate for inpatient claims, but there are problems with outpatient claims. Further analysis of problem areas might reveal that the problems are due to missing physician orders, outdated codes on the chargemaster, poor documentation, inadequate understanding of the procedure performed, or misunderstanding of the appropriate use of the affected codes. After the problems are identified, their causes can be determined and appropriate corrective actions instituted to prevent their recurrence.

Claim denial history and claims that have resulted in repeated overpayment should be examined, causes identified, and the most frequent sources of these denials and overpayments should be corrected.

Utilization of external data sources for benchmark comparison purposes is a good way to identify potential risk areas associated with current organizational coding practices. For instance, Medicare provider analysis and review (MEDPAR) data from CMS can be used to compare the distribution of diagnosis related groups (DRGs) for Medicare discharges. MEDPAR data are also available for skilled nursing facilities. CMS has a number of data files available on its Web site, including the MEDPAR data files. (See appendix G for fiscal year 2000 MEDPAR data for short-term, acute care hospitals, appendix F for a list of sources of comparative data, and appendix B for a list of risk areas being targeted by the OIG.)

Internal Coding Practices

Current written policies and procedures related to the coding of health data must be maintained. Coding policies establish the organization's guidelines to be followed in the coding process. If all of the organization's coding professionals follow the same set of clear, well-written guidelines, the organization will be more likely to achieve a higher level of coding consistency. Written policies and procedures pertaining to proper coding should reflect current regulatory requirements, including the following:

- The official coding guidelines promulgated by the Cooperating Parties (CMS, National Center for Health Statistics, American Hospital Association [AHA], and AHIMA)

- Current Procedural Terminology (CPT) rules promulgated by the American Medical Association (AMA)

- Uniform Hospital Discharge Data Set requirements (for acute care hospital inpatient hospitalizations)

- Requirements for uniform claims reporting established by the National Uniform Billing Committee and National Uniform Claims Committee

- Requirements for completion of patient assessment instruments (such as the PAI or OASIS)

- Individual payer policies

Coding Resources

Policies and procedures should identify the coding resources that are available to the coding staff. Essential coding resources include the following:

- Up-to-date International Classification of Diseases, Ninth Revision, Clinical Modification (ICD-9-CM); CPT; and Healthcare Common Procedure Coding System (HCPCS) codebooks

- Medical dictionary

- Anatomy/physiology textbook

- *Physicians' Desk Reference*

- Current subscription to AHA's *Coding Clinic for ICD-9-CM*

- Current subscription to AMA's *CPT Assistant*

- Current version of the National Correct Coding Initiative (CCI) manual

- Payers' reimbursement policies (for example, Medicare's Local Medical Review Policies and National Coverage Decisions)

- Payer bulletins and memoranda that affect the coding process

This list covers only the minimum requirements. Each organization should identify any additional coding resources that need be available to the coding staff.

These resources should be maintained in a location that is readily accessible to the coding staff. They should be kept in close proximity to the coding professionals' workstations and not in a private office (such as a supervisor's office) that sometimes may be inaccessible. The HIM compliance specialist should periodically (at least annually) check to ensure the availability and timeliness of the coding resources described in the policies and procedures. Using inappropriate or outdated coding resources places the organization at high risk for patterns of coding errors. In addition, the compliance program's effectiveness might be questioned if the organization was not relying on official or up-to-date coding resources (for example, allowing a subscription to *Coding Clinic for ICD-9-CM* to lapse). Even if an encoder is used, it remains important to provide access to current ICD-9-CM and CPT codebooks, because there may be times when coding personnel need to verify the appropriateness of an encoder code selection or edit.

The only official sources of coding advice and guidelines are the AHA for ICD-9-CM and the AMA for CPT. Although the healthcare organization may choose to subscribe to other vendors' coding publications for educational purposes, these are not considered official sources of coding advice and should not be relied on for verification of coding accuracy in the event of an audit or investigation.

Coding Process

Policies and procedures should describe the necessary steps the coding professional should take during the course of reviewing a health record. Direction also should be provided on the proper steps to take in those situations when an official source does not provide guidance (for example, when neither the codebook nor *Coding Clinic for ICD-9-CM* provides direction on the most appropriate ICD-9-CM code for a stated diagnosis or procedure).

To ensure consistency, coding policies and procedures should identify the optional codes the organization wishes to collect (such as morphology codes or procedure codes that are not required for reporting purposes). The organization's use of E codes should be described.

Facility-Specific Coding Guidelines

Facility-specific coding guidelines should be developed for situations that are not addressed by the official coding rules and guidelines. HIM professionals can work together with their medical staff to develop coding guidelines that promote complete documentation needed for consistent code assignment. Specific and detailed coding guidelines that cover the reporting of typical services provided by the organization create tools for data consistency and reliability by ensuring that all coding staff interpret clinical documentation and apply coding principles in the same manner. These guidelines can reveal to the coding professionals the circumstances when they should query physicians for clarification of documentation. The coding guidelines should be specific to the settings to which they apply. An example of a situation that might warrant a facility-specific guideline is an unusual diagnosis or a new procedure for which there is no official instruction regarding the appropriate code assignment. In this situation, the issue must be researched to ensure that the diagnosis or procedure has not been previously addressed by an official source of coding advice. If it has not been addressed, the issue should be submitted, along with appropriate health record documentation, to the proper source for determination of an official answer. Publication of an official answer will ensure consistency in coding because all healthcare providers will be using the same code when they encounter this diagnosis or procedure. In the meantime, while waiting for an official answer, the coder may consult the attending physician for direction on the most appropriate code, solicit buy-in on this code selection by other physicians on the medical staff who are likely to encounter the same diagnosis or procedure, and develop a facility-specific guideline for application of this code whenever this diagnosis or procedure is encountered.

Another example of a situation when facility-specific guidelines are appropriate is the development of clinical criteria, through collaboration of coding staff and physicians, for determining the circumstances when querying the physician is appropriate (see Practice Brief: Developing a Physician Query Process in appendix D). The appropriate medical staff committee should give final approval of any facility-specific coding guidelines that involve clinical criteria to assure appropriateness and physician consensus.

Facility-specific guidelines must be applied consistently to all records coded. They should not be developed to replace the physician documentation needed to support code assignment. *Facility-specific coding guidelines must not conflict with official rules and guidelines.* Once official advice addressing the situation has been received, the organization-specific guideline is invalidated and should no longer be used. If the facility-specific guidelines are maintained electronically, they should be searchable by key terms. Placing guidelines on a facility intranet or internal computer network is an efficient way to ensure their accessibility and consistent use and also enables timely and efficient updating and distribution. If the computer network permits access to the Internet, live links can be incorporated to Web sites containing regulatory requirements related to documentation, claims submission, and code assignment.

Clarification of Coding Advice

When ambiguity or conflicting advice regarding a coding or reimbursement issue exists, official sources should be contacted for clarification and all responses should be documented. All supporting and relevant data relating to the coding, documentation, or billing issue should be retrieved. A summary document outlining all sources contacted, responses, and clarification and instructions obtained should be prepared. Depending on the nature of the issue, it may be appropriate to do one of the following:

- Research the *Federal Register,* fiscal intermediary/carrier bulletins, CMS program memoranda or transmittals

- Visit a government, fiscal intermediary/carrier, or private payer Web site

- Contact a professional association such as AHIMA, AHA, AMA, Healthcare Financial Management Association (HFMA), or Medical Group Management Association (MGMA)

Coding Accuracy Standards

Healthcare organizations should establish their own acceptable coding accuracy standards. These standards should be based on each organization's unique characteristics and realistic expectations with consideration given to standards that are reasonable and yet minimize the risk of erroneous claims submission.

Claims Denials and Rejections

An organizational policy and procedure should be developed for processing claims denials and rejections. All rejected or denied claims pertaining to a diagnostic or procedural coding issue must be returned to the coding staff for review and, if necessary, code correction. If the claim pertains to the chargemaster, it should be forwarded to the affected ancillary department for review and resolution.

The business office generally receives claim denials and rejection but may not share those involving coding issues with the HIM department. As a result, coding personnel may not be aware that code assignments have caused claim denials or delays. Staff from the appropriate departments should work together in identifying rejections and denials, tracking denial trends, and taking corrective action. Organizational policy should emphasize that diagnosis and procedure codes, including modifiers, should never be changed by billing personnel without the consensus of the department that assigned the original codes. If there is disagreement between the coding and billing staff, the issue should be referred to the coding supervisor. If necessary, the coding supervisor should forward it to the HIM compliance specialist or, if this position does not exist, to the corporate compliance officer.

When an error in code assignment or a discrepancy between the code(s) reported by the coding staff and the code(s) submitted on the claim is discovered after claim submission, the organization should implement its established process for updating and correcting the information system and amending or correcting the claim.

Requests to Change Codes

A policy and procedure should be established for handling patient and physician requests to inappropriately change codes to codes that the patient's insurance will reimburse. The policies and procedures should stipulate that codes will not be assigned, modified, or excluded solely for the purpose of maximizing reimbursement. Codes should not be changed or amended due to the request of the physician, patient, or member of the patient's family in order to have the service covered by the patient's health insurance. If the initial code assignment did not accurately reflect the service provided or the reason for the service, the code(s) may be revised based on supporting documentation. Disputes with physicians or patients regarding coding issues should be handled by the coding manager and appropriately logged for review.

Disputes with Physicians

Appropriate methods for resolving coding or documentation disputes with physicians should also be described in the organization's HIM policies and procedures. For example, the issue might be referred to a physician liaison or a medical staff committee for resolution. If the final outcome is such that the organization faces a compliance risk (for example, the attending physician absolutely refuses to allow a code to be reported in compliance with an official coding guideline), detailed documentation of the issue, including all steps taken to attempt to resolve it, should be maintained. Figure 2 (see page 14) provides a list of suggested internal coding practices that the healthcare organization may wish to specifically address in its HIM compliance program.

Documentation Requirements

Policies and procedures should address appropriate documentation requirements. Documentation of all physician and other professional services should be proper (that is, according to regulatory standards and generally accepted documentation practices), complete, and timely to ensure that only accurate and properly documented services are billed.

Claims should be submitted only when appropriate documentation supporting them is present in the health record and available for audit and review. Processes for ensuring that health record documentation is adequate and appropriate to support the coded diagnoses and procedures need to be in place. When evaluating the appropriateness of documentation, the following questions should be asked:

- Is the chief complaint and/or reason for the patient encounter or hospitalization documented?
- Do the initial orders for patient care reflect the level of care to be provided?
- Is there an appropriate history and physical examination?

Figure 2. Guidelines for HIM policy and procedure development

Guideline 1

Responses to the following questions should be considered for inclusion in the healthcare organization's policies and procedures. These represent suggestions only and are not intended to be all-inclusive.

- What is the organization's process for coding a health record?
- What is the appropriate course of action coding professionals should take when a coding situation is not explicitly addressed in official coding guidelines?
- What is the appropriate course of action when the coding professional notes abnormal test results or other findings on a report in an acute care, hospital, inpatient record that have not been addressed in the physician documentation?
- What is the appropriate course of action when the coding professional notes a definitive diagnosis on a physician interpretation of a diagnostic test performed during an outpatient encounter?
- What is the appropriate course of action when the coding professional notes abnormal test results on a report of a diagnostic test that does not have a physician interpretation, performed during an outpatient encounter?
- What is the appropriate course of action when inconsistent or conflicting documentation appears in the health record?
- What is the appropriate process for querying a physician to clarify a diagnosis or procedure and ensuring that the physician adds any necessary information to the health record?
- What is the proper method for amending health record documentation or adding information to the health record after conclusion of the patient encounter?
- What is the mechanism for resolving disputes with physicians? (One option is to use a physician advisor who can provide guidance to coding professionals on clinical issues and serve as a liaison between coding professionals and physicians.)
- What is the process for resolving coding questions or disagreements (with other coding professionals, supervisors, payers, consultants, and so on)? (It may be desirable to assign a staff member responsibility for dispute resolution. If there is no impact on reimbursement, this individual might be a coding supervisor; however, for issues affecting reimbursement, this responsibility might be given to the HIM compliance specialist.)
- What is the appropriate course of action when the service being coded involves a new device or technology that has not yet been addressed in the classification system?
- What is the appropriate course of action if a code cannot be assigned for any reason?

Guideline 2

The following additional areas should also be covered in the organization's policies and procedures.

- Policy for handling recommendations made by a nonofficial source (seminar instructor, consultant, or other source):

  —If a recommendation or coding practice seems questionable, references or resources supporting it should be requested.

  —No recommendation or coding practice that conflicts with official coding rules/guidelines, regulations, and payment policies should be implemented.

- Clear statement of the organization's commitment to adhere to official coding rules and guidelines
- Any facility-specific coding guidelines the organization has developed to assist coding personnel with proper code selection and to promote internal consistency

  —Facility-specific guidelines must not conflict with coding system rules and conventions or official guidelines.

- Payer policies pertaining to reporting of diagnosis and procedure codes

Organizations may wish to incorporate recommendations from AHIMA practice briefs and other publications (see appendix D for a few of the pertinent AHIMA practice briefs).

Figure 2. *(Continued)*

Guideline 3

The organization's policies and procedures should address the use of encoders or other computer software.

- The organization should not rely solely on encoding software for code assignment. The encoder may not include all of the information found in the code books. To verify codes, notes, cross-references, and other conventions and instructions, up-to-date ICD-9-CM and CPT codebooks should be readily available.

- If the encoder permits customized edits, utilize them for coding rules or guidelines that are difficult to remember. For payment policies affecting code assignment, payer-specific edits might be incorporated in the encoder to help coding professionals remember the policy.

- Coding staff should familiarize themselves with the annual ICD-9-CM addendum and CPT code revisions so they are able to identify errors in encoder software.

- Coding staff should be educated to detect inappropriate logic or errors in encoding software. Procedures for addressing perceived errors in logic or inappropriate edits in encoder, billing, or other types of software should be developed. Suggested steps to follow when a possible error is identified include:

  —Coding staff should immediately report the issue to the coding manager and it should be reported to the vendor promptly.

  —If the software error is an unequivocal conflict with official coding rules and guidelines, immediate corrective action should be implemented. Coding staff should be informed of erroneous instruction and directed to disregard software instruction; and if software permits customized edits, an edit should be developed to remind coding staff of the error and the appropriate code assignment.

  —Follow-up with the vendor should be done on a regular basis until the issue has been satisfactorily resolved.

  —All communication with vendor should be documented, including organizational inquiries and vendor responses.

  —All software errors should be documented, including the date the error was detected and how it was handled, and the date it was resolved. This documentation should be kept with the coding policies and procedures.

  —If the error resulted in an overpayment by a payer, every reasonable effort should be made to identify overpaid claims and return the overpayment to the respective payer (with a letter of explanation).

  —Software logic or edit errors affecting reimbursement should be reported to the HIM compliance specialist, who then should report it to the corporate compliance officer.

Guideline 4

The organization's policies and procedures should also address chargemaster maintenance. The importance of ongoing maintenance of the chargemaster is critical, because many factors that go into the chargemaster are constantly changing, such as annual updates to CPT/HCPCS codes, changes in reimbursement policies, updates to charges, growth in outpatient services, advances in technology, and development of new service lines. A minimum of one review per year of the chargemaster should be undertaken to ensure that it is accurate, complete, and up-to-date with code revisions and regulatory changes. Ideally, chargemaster maintenance should not be the responsibility of one person but, rather, should be overseen by a committee composed of representatives from ancillary departments, billing, and HIM. Proper chargemaster maintenance requires expertise in coding, billing regulations, and health record documentation requirements. An HIM representative should always be involved in the updating of chargemaster programs.

- Are all services that were provided documented?

- Does documentation clearly explain why support services, procedures, and supplies were provided?

- Is assessment of the patient's condition included in the documentation?

- Does documentation include information on the patient's progress and treatment outcome?

- Is there a documented treatment plan?

- Does the plan for care include, as appropriate, treatments and medications (including frequency and dosage), any referrals and consultations, patient and family education, and follow-up instructions?

- Are changes to the treatment plan, including rationale, documented?

- Is there documentation of medical rationale for services rendered?

- Does documentation support standards for medical necessity?

- Are abnormal test results addressed in the physician documentation?

- Are relevant health risk factors identified?

- Does documentation support intensity of patient evaluation and/or treatment, including thought processes and complexity of decision making?

- Are significant changes in the patient's condition and action taken documented?

- Is the status of unresolved problems documented?

- Is planned follow-up care documented?

- Does documentation support the level of care provided?

- Does documentation meet the criteria for the evaluation and management code billed?

- Does the documentation for the patient encounter include an assessment, clinical impression, or diagnosis?

- Are all diagnoses and procedurs documented as specifically as possible?

- Do clinical reports include all elements required by regulatory and accreditation agencies?

- Are necessary health record entries dated and authenticated?

The level of care to be provided should be clearly documented in the initial orders. For example, simply documenting "admit" is confusing because it is not clear if the patient is to be admitted as an inpatient, for outpatient surgery, or to outpatient observation. The order for level of care should be explicitly documented, such as "admit as inpatient," "admit to outpatient surgery," or "admit to observation."

Health records should be organized and legible so they can be coded accurately and readily audited. Documentation that should be available at the time of coding should be specifically described in the organization's policies and procedures. No federal requirement exists on the specific health record documents that must be present when the health record is coded. However, the *OIG's Compliance Program Guidance for Hospitals* states "that the documentation necessary for accurate code assignment should be available to coding staff" (OIG 1998, p. 8991). Therefore, if an organization chooses to exclude certain reports from having to be available at the time of coding (such as the discharge summary, certain consultation reports, the operative report, or complete office note documentation), and it is ultimately determined that one of these reports contains information affecting code assignment (and that information is not present elsewhere in the health record), this may be viewed as evidence of noncompliance. If one's organizational policy allows the coding of incomplete records, a process needs to be developed to ensure the record and codes are re-reviewed once the record is complete to ensure the additional documentation does not change the code assignments. If the codes do need to be changed and the claim has already been submitted, the claim will need to be rebilled with the correct codes.

Standards for the timely completion of health records stipulated in the medical staff bylaws or policies should be adhered to. In addition to addressing requirements from regulatory agencies (for example, Joint Commission on Accreditation of Healthcare Organizations [JCAHO]), the healthcare organization's standards for health record completion should take into consideration the documentation necessary for coding. Health record completion standards should reasonably ensure that unnecessary delays in the coding process are not inadvertently built into the record completion process. Ideally, services should be documented at the time the service is provided or as soon afterward as is practical.

In addition to considering the timely completion of report dictation by clinicians, the timeliness of the transcription and filing of dictated reports should be addressed.

If organizational policies allow for coding of incomplete health records, a procedure should be in place to ensure that those records are reviewed after the record is complete. This includes ensuring that the information contained in handwritten reports is consistent with transcribed reports, if the coding staff relied upon handwritten reports during the coding process. Alternate methods of accessing information necessary for coding, which may obviate the need to wait for completion of the health record, should be considered. For example, the necessary information may be available electronically.

Physician Query Process

Codes should be based on physician documentation. Physician documentation is the cornerstone of accurate coding. Documentation is not limited to the face sheet, discharge summary, progress notes, history and physical, or other report designed to capture diagnostic information. Ensuring the accuracy of coded data is a shared responsibility between coding professionals and physicians. Accurate diagnostic and procedural coded data originate from collaboration between physicians, who have a clinical background, and coding professionals, who have an understanding of classification systems. If evidence of a diagnosis exists in the health record and the coding professional is uncertain whether it is a valid diagnosis because the documentation is incomplete, unclear, or contradictory, then it is the coding professional's responsibility to query the attending physician to determine if this diagnosis should be coded and reported.

Healthcare organizations should establish a mechanism for obtaining physician clarification. For example, the policies and procedures might include a statement authorizing the coding professionals to contact a physician directly regarding a record he or she is coding. This will clarify that communication with physicians is not restricted to supervisory personnel.

Policies regarding the circumstances when physicians will be queried should be designed to promote complete and accurate coding and complete documentation. The process of querying physicians is an effective and necessary mechanism for improving the quality of coding and health record documentation and capturing complete clinical data. Query forms must be used as a communication tool meant to improve the accuracy of code assignments and the quality of physician documentation, not to inappropriately maximize reimbursement. It would be inappropriate to implement a policy requiring that the physician be queried only when reimbursement is affected, as such a policy will skew national healthcare data and could lead to charges of upcoding.

Patterns of physician documentation problems (for example, use of the term *urosepsis* without indicating whether the patient has a urinary tract infection or septicemia), whether for an individual physician or across all physicians, should be addressed in physician educational programs and monitored to determine if the problem is resolved or has lessened. If no improvement is noted after a predetermined time period, corrective action should be initiated. (See Practice Brief: Developing a Physician Query Process in appendix D.)

The healthcare organization may wish to designate a physician to provide guidance to the coding staff on clinical issues and to serve as a liaison with the medical staff. Appendix C offers sample communication tools for improving physician documentation.

Payment Policies

Organizations should document their efforts to comply with applicable statutes, regulations, and federal healthcare program requirements. When advice is requested from a government agency (including a Medicare fiscal intermediary or carrier) charged with administering a federal healthcare program, a record of the request and any written or oral response must be documented and retained. A log of oral inquiries between the organization and third parties (government and private entities) will help document the organization's compliance efforts. These records could become relevant in a subsequent investigation to the issue of whether the organization's reliance on this advice was reasonable and whether it exercised due diligence in developing procedures and practices to implement the advice.

Payment policies affecting code assignment should be incorporated into coding policies and procedures. A copy of the provider bulletin or any other official memorandum addressing payment policy should be filed with the policies and procedures so that the organization will be able to produce documentation supporting the coding practice. Should the payer provide advice or direction on a particular policy verbally, the organization should request that information in writing. If the organization's encoder allows customized edits, payer-specific edits for the code(s) affected by a payer policy should be created. With respect to Medicare, information concerning specific payment policies should be available from the Medicare contractor under the Freedom of Information Act. This information may also be posted on the CMS or the Medicare contractor's Web site. If attempts to obtain the information in writing are unsuccessful, the conversation with the payer should be documented, including the date(s), name(s) of the individuals involved in the conversation(s), and the provider organization's interpretation of the payer's advice. A copy should be faxed to the payer along with a request that the payer representative sign the document and fax it back. Finally, a copy of the confirmation that the fax was successfully delivered should be kept on file. Another method is to send a letter to the payer via certified mail and request a reply if the payer does not concur with the summary of the conversation. Even if the payer fails to provide its advice in writing, sign the summary of the discussion, or reply to the certified letter, the provider organization will still have evidence that a summary of the conversation was provided to the payer. This documentation should be kept in the policy and procedure manual.

When submitting a claim for reimbursement, payment policies take precedence. If a payer has a policy that clearly conflicts with official coding rules or guidelines, every effort should be made to resolve the issue with the payer. First, determine whether the issue is related to coding or coverage. For example, the denial may be referred to the HIM department with a message from the business office that the claim was denied because code V72.5, Radiology examination, was an unacceptable diagnosis. Many insurance policies do not include coverage for routine services (such as annual physical examinations and screening tests) and this code is assigned when the patient has no signs or symptoms. Therefore, the denial may really be related to noncoverage of the service provided rather than the accuracy of the reported code.

If it is determined that the problem is not related to a coverage issue and does involve a conflict between a payer requirement and the official coding rules or guidelines, the payer should be contacted and an attempt made to explain the problem. For example, a letter could be sent to the payer (in the case of Medicare, to the fiscal intermediary or carrier) pointing out the conflict and the problems it could cause with data consistency and comparability. The applicable coding rule or guideline should be included. (AHIMA's *Payer's Guide to Healthcare Diagnostic and Procedural Data Quality,* available at www.ahima.org, may be used as a tool to support the organization's position and the underlying rationale.) If the payer involved is Medicare and no satisfactory resolution is achieved with the Medicare contractor, the appropriate CMS regional office should be contacted. An organization's business office or Medicare contractor can provide contact information for the CMS regional office with jurisdiction in one's particular area.

If the payer refuses to change its policy, an attempt should be made to obtain its policy in writing. If the payer refuses to provide the policy in writing, all conversations with the payer should be documented, including dates, names of individuals involved, and the substance of the discussion. Furthermore, the payment policy should be confirmed by a representative of the payer's management. A file should be kept of all documentation on communications with the payer regarding this issue.

If it seems that the Medicare contractor is interpreting CMS policy incorrectly, the organization should work with the contractor to resolve the issue. If necessary, the CMS regional office may need to be involved. The organization may also wish to solicit assistance from its state hospital association. If the issue appears to be relatively broad in scope (that is, involving multiple Medicare contractors), soliciting AHIMA's assistance to resolve the issue at a national level should be considered.

Health Insurance Portability and Accountability Act

An organization's HIM compliance program should address compliance with all of the regulations promulgated under the Health Insurance Portability and Accountability Act (HIPAA). At press time, final regulations pertaining to electronic transactions and code sets and privacy of individually identifiable health information had been published, but full implementation was not yet required.

Standards for Electronic Transactions and Code Sets

HIPAA requires the adoption of standards for code sets for data elements that are part of all healthcare transactions. The regulation pertaining to electronic transactions and code sets promulgated under HIPAA named the following standard code sets:

- ICD-9-CM volumes 1 and 2 are to be used in all healthcare settings to report diseases, injuries, impairments, and other health problems and their manifestations.

- ICD-9-CM volume 3 is to be used for acute care hospital inpatient services to report procedures or other actions taken to prevent, diagnose, treat, and manage diseases, injuries, and impairments.

- A combination of CPT and HCPCS is to be used to report physician and other healthcare services.

- HCPCS is to be used for all other substances, equipment, supplies, or other items used in healthcare services.

- Current Dental Terminology (CDT) is to be used for dental services.

- The National Drug Code (NDC) is to be used for drugs and biologics (at press time, it was expected that this standard would be modified to allow HCPCS codes to be reported for drugs and biologics by entities other than retail pharmacies)

The standard code sets include both the codes and modifiers, if the code set contains modifiers. Although HIPAA does not require payers to reimburse for all valid codes within the standard code sets, payers are required to accept all valid codes within a standard code set. The version of the code set that is valid at the time healthcare services are furnished must be used by both providers and payers.

For ICD-9-CM, HIPAA requires both providers and payers to adhere to the *Official ICD-9-CM Guidelines for Coding and Reporting.* Operational guidelines and instructions are not included as part of the other standard code sets.

The compliance date for implementation of the code sets and transaction standards is October 16, 2002, for providers and health plans other than small health plans. Small plans must comply by October 16, 2003. However, subsequent legislation allows a covered provider or health plan to obtain a one-year delay if the provider or plan submits a compliance plan to the Secretary of Health and Human Services by October 16, 2002, containing the following:

- An analysis reflecting the extent to which and the reasons why they are not in compliance

- A budget, schedule, work plan, and implementation strategy for achieving compliance

- Whether the entity plans to use or might use a contractor or other vendor to assist in achieving compliance

- A time frame for testing that begins no later than April 16, 2003

Compliance and the HIPAA Privacy Rule

The final regulation for the standards for privacy of individually identifiable health information promulgated under HIPAA requires covered entities to designate a privacy official who is responsible for the development and implementation of policies and procedures relative to privacy. To be considered a covered entity that is required to comply with the privacy rule, a health plan, healthcare clearinghouse, or healthcare provider must utilize at least one of the standardized transactions under HIPAA. The rule stipulates that covered entities are required to train all members of its workforce on the policies and procedures with respect to protected health information.

According to AHIMA's sample privacy officer job description, the privacy officer is responsible for oversight of "all ongoing activities related to the development, implementation, maintenance of, and adherence to the organization's policies and procedures covering the privacy of, and access to, patient health information in compliance with federal and state laws and the healthcare organization's information privacy practices" (Help 2001, p. 37). Specific responsibilities identified in the sample job description that illustrate the correlation between compliance with reimbursement regulations and requirements and compliance with the federal privacy rule include the following (Help 2001, pp. 37–38):

- Provides development guidance and assists in the identification, implementation, and maintenance of the organization information privacy policies and procedures in coordination with the organization management and administration, the privacy oversight committee, and legal counsel

- Works with organization senior management and corporate compliance officer to establish an organization-wide privacy oversight committee . . .

- Performs initial and periodic information privacy risk assessments and conducts related ongoing compliance monitoring activities in coordination with the [organization's] other compliance and operational assessment functions . . .

- Oversees, directs, delivers, or ensures delivery of initial and [ongoing] privacy training and orientation to all employees, volunteers, medical and professional staff, contractors, alliances, business associates, and other appropriate third parties . . .

- Maintains current knowledge of applicable federal and state privacy laws and accreditation standards and monitors advancements in information privacy technologies to ensure organizational adaptation and compliance

- Serves as information privacy consultant to the organization for all departments and appropriate entities . . .

HIM professionals are uniquely qualified to assume the role of privacy officials because they fulfill the following responsibilities (AHIMA 2001):

- Interpret state and federal laws that apply to the use of health information [and translate them] into policy

- Understand the decision-making processes throughout healthcare that rely on information

- Direct the flow of information within healthcare organizations and throughout healthcare

- Apply HIM principles to information in all its forms

- Understand the content of health information in its clinical, research, and business contexts

- Apply the technologies used to collect, access, store, and transmit information in all its forms

- Establish and recognize best practices in the management of privacy of health information

- Collaborate with other healthcare professionals to ensure appropriate security measures are in place

- Historically, managed the release of information function

- Establish policy, train staff, develop consents, release information, and document information use

- Advocate for the patient, relative to health information confidentiality

- Live by a professional Code of Ethics specific to maintenance of patient privacy

Since the primary responsibilities for both the privacy official and the individual responsible for HIM compliance both involve oversight of regulatory compliance related to health information management, some organizations may decide to charge one individual with both sets of responsibilities. However, depending on the organizational size and structure, this may not be feasible. Also, due to the differences in skill sets related to privacy and coding expertise, the individual most qualified for the HIM compliance specialist may not be the individual most qualified to serve as the privacy official. In any case, it is imperative that the individual or individuals charged with oversight for compliance with reimbursement regulations and policies and for compliance with the privacy regulations are not overburdened with a myriad of responsibilities and have sufficient resources to be effective. Even if an organization decides that the responsibilities are too great for a single individual to assume, it may choose to link these roles through a reporting relationship (for example, both positions might report to the same individual or department). Certain functions of both roles may also appropriately be consolidated. For example, it may be appropriate to develop training programs that address both privacy issues and compliance with reimbursement regulations.

Medical Necessity

Medicare, as well as most other payers, will not pay for any items or services it does not consider to be reasonable and necessary for the diagnosis or treatment of illness or injury or to improve the functioning of a malformed body member. The first step in determining medical necessity is to determine whether the payer considers the services as covered or noncovered. Services that are classified as noncovered by a payer are never reimbursed by that payer, regardless of the diagnosis or circumstance.

Covered services can be judged to be either medically necessary or unnecessary. For certain services, Medicare has issued national coverage decisions that explain when an item or service will be considered medically necessary and, thus, eligible for Medicare coverage. National coverage decisions apply nationwide and are binding on all Medicare contractors, quality improvement organizations (QIOs, formerly known as peer review organizations [PROs]), health maintenance organizations, competitive medical plans, and health care prepayment plans for purposes of Medicare coverage. In the absence of a specific national coverage decision, coverage decisions are made at the discretion of the Medicare contractors. The contractors develop local medical review policies (LMRPs) that explain when an item or service will (or will not) be considered *reasonable and necessary* and thus eligible (or ineligible) for Medicare coverage. According to the Medicare Program Integrity Manual, Medicare contractors must develop medical review policies for services that have one or more of the following characteristics:

- Are being furnished to an extent that raises questions of abuse or overutilization

- Appear to have been furnished under conditions inconsistent with standards of practice or accepted technology

- Appear not to be medically reasonable and necessary

Contractors develop these LMRPs by considering medical literature, the advice of local medical societies and medical consultants, and public comments. An LMRP applies only within the area it serves. An LMRP may not conflict with a national coverage decision once the national coverage decision becomes effective. If a national coverage decision conflicts with a previously-established LMRP, the contractor must change its LMRP to conform to the national coverage decision. A contractor may develop an LMRP that supplements a national coverage decision where the national coverage decision is silent on an issue. The LMRP may not alter the national coverage decision. Both national coverage decisions and LMRPs generally include a narrative section describing the indications for the item or service and a list of ICD-9-CM diagnosis codes that support, or do not support, medical necessity of the item or service. (LMRPs for all Medicare contractors are available at www.lmrp.net.)

Private payers also develop specific coverage policies and may use differing definitions of *medical necessity.*

Because medical necessity is determined by the ICD-9-CM diagnosis code(s) describing the patient's symptom(s) or condition(s) necessitating the service, accurate code assignment is critical. Due to the need to establish medical necessity prior to rendering care, this coding may be performed by individuals who have not received adequate coding education and training, resulting in inaccurate (or incorrect) code assignments. Also, missing, incomplete, or unclear documentation from the physician ordering the service can lead to coding inaccuracies.

Documentation to Support Medical Necessity

The Balanced Budget Act of 1997 requires physicians and qualified nonphysician practitioners to provide diagnostic information when ordering services furnished by another entity when the Medicare contractor has an LMRP requiring such diagnostic information from the entity performing the service. This diagnostic information must be provided at the time the item or service is ordered. While Medicare may not require ordering physicians and nonphysician practitioners to provide diagnostic information in every instance, it is highly recommended that organizations require physicians and nonphysician practices to provide diagnostic information each time they order items or services. This policy will be administratively simpler, ensure consistent documentation practices, and lessen confusion as to when diagnostic information is necessary. The ordering physician or practitioner should provide this information in narrative form, and the trained HIM coding staff at the organization performing the diagnostic test(s) should translate it to ICD-9-CM code(s). If tests are ordered electronically, the diagnosis field should be a mandatory field. If hard-copy requisition forms are used, the field for the diagnosis should be prominent and the form should contain a reminder about the necessity to document the reason for the test on the form. The entity performing the service must maintain the documentation that it receives from the ordering physician or qualified nonphysician practitioner. The ordering physician or qualified nonphysician practitioner must maintain documentation of medical necessity in the patient's health record. Upon request by CMS, the provider performing the test and submitting the claim for the service must be able to provide documentation of the order for the service billed (including sufficient information to enable CMS to identify and contact the ordering physician or nonphysician practitioner), documentation showing accurate processing of the order and submission of the claim, and diagnostic or other medical information supplied by the ordering physician or nonphysician practitioner.

Medicare regulations require that diagnostic X-ray tests, diagnostic laboratory tests, and other diagnostic tests must be ordered by the physician who is treating the patient for a specific medical problem and who uses the results in the management of the patient's specific medical problem. CMS has indicated that this requirement does not necessarily mean that there must be a physician's signature on the test requisition. However, documentation that the physician or nonphysician practitioner ordered the test must be available upon CMS's request. According to CMS, while the signature of a physician on the requisition is one way of documenting that the treating physician has ordered the test, it is not the only permissible way of documenting that the treating physician ordered the test. For example, the treating physician may document the ordering of specific tests in the patient's health record. The Medicare Carrier Manual defines an order for a diagnostic test as a communication from the treating physician or practitioner requesting that a diagnostic test be performed on a patient. In a CMS Program Memorandum AB-01-144 (2001), CMS has indicated that an order may include the following forms of communication:

- A written document signed by the treating physician/practitioner, which is hand-delivered, mailed, or faxed to the testing facility

- A telephone call by the treating physician/practitioner or his/her office to the testing facility

- An electronic mail by the treating physician/practitioner or his/her office to the testing facility

For orders communicated via telephone, CMS requires both the treating physician/practitioner and the testing facility to document the telephone call in their respective copies of the patient's health record. Organizations' medical staff rules and regulations should address the policy and procedure for processing telephone orders and indicate who is authorized to receive them.

Documentation supporting medical necessity of the service rendered should be maintained in the patient's health record (at the organization performing the diagnostic tests) and should be legible. The provider performing the service may request additional diagnostic and other medical information to document that the services performed are medically necessary. In the event that there is no diagnosis on the physician's order and the coding staff must contact his or her office for the diagnostic information pertaining to the ordered services, this information should be obtained only from the physician or a designated member of his or her office staff. Where diagnostic information is obtained from a physician or his or her staff after receipt of the specimen and request for services, it should be documented by the HIM staff, including the diagnosis supporting the diagnostic test, the date the information was obtained, and the name of the individual providing the information. This information should be maintained in the patient's health record. The organization's policies and procedures should stipulate the specific location in the health record where maintenance of this information should occur.

Although CMS allows organizations to obtain diagnostic information as to the reason a test is being performed directly from the patient (per Program Memorandum AB-01-144), in the event that the ordering physician/practitioner has not supplied the information and is unavailable, this practice is not recommended. Patients may not accurately describe the reason for the test or they may describe the reason in nonmedical terms, which then must be translated into clinical terms by staff, and their description of the reason for the test may not be supported by health record documentation. When no diagnostic information is provided by the ordering physician/practitioner and he is unavailable, it may be preferable to issue an advance beneficiary notice (ABN) than to rely on diagnostic information provided by the patient. Prior to submitting the claim, the ordering physician/practitioner should be contacted for diagnostic information.

Instances when diagnostic information supporting tests must be obtained after the fact should be the exception rather than the norm. Physicians should be expected to provide the necessary diagnostic information at the time the service is ordered. The HIM department should monitor physician compliance to identify patterns. When a pattern of noncompliance by a particular physician is identified, appropriate corrective action should be taken. This might include targeted education, refusal to perform tests in the future until diagnostic information has been obtained, or initiating penalties for repeated noncompliance. Patterns that should be closely monitored include lack of provision of any diagnostic information on the test requisition, provision of unacceptable diagnostic information (such as a rule-out diagnosis without specification of the patient's symptoms), provision of diagnoses that do not meet Medicare's definition of medical necessity (as defined in LMRPs), and no issuance of an ABN. In cases where there is a recurring pattern of noncompliance, organizational policy should delineate appropriate disciplinary action.

Ideally, periodic, random reviews of physicians' office records for those cases where diagnostic information was provided verbally to coding staff should be conducted to ascertain that the information provided is documented appropriately. However, physicians' practices that are not owned by the healthcare organization are not required to permit the organization access to their records. These reviews can only be conducted if the physicians grant their consent. When patterns of problems are identified, education should be provided to the physicians whose office documentation is found to be inadequate.

If a provider believes that an ICD-9-CM code has been inadvertently omitted from a payer's coverage policy, or an appropriate diagnosis is not included in the indications for the item or service, the issue should be brought to the attention of the respective payer, along with documentation to support the inclusion of the code or diagnosis. Medicare contractors are required to solicit public comments on their draft LMRPs. They generally accomplish this by posting their draft LMRPs on their Web site, publishing them in bulletins, and holding advisory committee meetings that are open to the public. It is important for HIM professionals to review these draft policies and ensure that the listed ICD-9-CM codes are complete and accurate and consistent with coding rules and guidelines. HIM professionals are also encouraged to actively seek ongoing involvement in the development of LMRPs, through volunteering to serve on the local Medicare contractor's advisory committee or attending all advisory committee meetings. Any identified errors in the listed codes or missing codes should be brought to the attention of the payer. This will ensure that providers can receive the appropriate reimbursement for the item or service without being required to violate coding rules and guidelines. The importance of ensuring that coverage policies are consistent with ICD-9-CM coding rules and guidelines in light of the HIPAA requirement for adherence to the *Official ICD-9-CM Guidelines for Coding and Reporting* should be stressed to payers. During the process of reviewing draft coverage policies, input from physicians should also be sought to ensure that the clinical indications for the item or service are complete and accurate. It is important for the narrative indications stated in a coverage policy to be consistent with the ICD-9-CM codes that support medical necessity.

Advance Beneficiary Notices

If the healthcare provider has reason to believe that Medicare will deny an item or service because Medicare's coverage criteria have not been met, an advance beneficiary notice (ABN) should be issued to the Medicare patient or his or her legal representative before performing the test. An example of such an instance is when the physician's reason for ordering a diagnostic test or therapy services for a Medicare beneficiary does not meet Medicare's medical necessity standards. The ABN relieves the provider of the item or service of liability because the notice is proof of the beneficiary's prior knowledge of the likelihood of noncoverage. It also allows the provider to collect payment for the item or service from the patient if Medicare denies the claim. An ABN must be signed by the patient after the service is ordered and before it has been performed. Each ABN should meet the following requirements:

- Be expressed in writing

- Identify the specific service that may be denied

- State the specific reason why the physician believes the service may be denied

- Be signed by the patient (when another person signs for the patient, the name and relationship to the patient should be documented) acknowledging that the required information was provided and that the patient assumes responsibility for paying for the service

An ABN will not be considered acceptable if the patient is asked to sign a blank form. An ABN should never be issued routinely without regard to a particular need, as the ABN must state the specific reason the physician anticipates that the particular service will not be reimbursed. Each time diagnostic information is missing on the test requisition, an ABN should not be routinely issued to the patient in lieu of contacting the ordering physician for a diagnosis. This practice could be construed as routine issuance of ABNs, which is prohibited by Medicare.

Although the ABN may be issued by either the organization providing the item or service or the physician ordering it, the organization must produce a copy of the ABN upon Medicare's request. Also, the organization that billed for the item or service will not be protected from liability if at least one of the following is true:

- The provider of the item or service believes the physician issued an ABN but in actuality he did not

- The ABN issued by the physician is unacceptable to Medicare (for example, it does not contain all of the information required by Medicare or was not issued before the service was provided)

- The physician's office cannot locate the ABN (and the provider of the item or service does not have a copy)

However, if the physician is charged with responsibility for issuing the ABN, his or her knowledge of Medicare's medical necessity standards is continuously reinforced and he or she is more likely to keep these standards in mind when ordering diagnostic tests. This also places the burden of explaining to a Medicare patient why a test is being ordered that Medicare considers medically unnecessary on the ordering physician, which is where this responsibility belongs. If the physician is responsible for issuing the ABN, a copy of the notice should be attached to the test requisition or order form and sent to the organization providing and billing for the item or service. This ensures the organization that the ABN has been issued and meets Medicare requirements.

Medical Necessity Screening Software

Some facilities utilize screening software to check for medical necessity. Medical necessity software applications supply information to providers regarding whether a particular service (represented as a CPT code) will be covered by Medicare based on the ICD-9-CM diagnosis codes identified in the applicable LMRP. Most LMRPs contain examples of covered and noncovered ICD-9-CM codes, but in many situations a service would meet medical necessity criteria based on the narrative indications for the test described in the LMRP that are not explicitly identified by the ICD-9-CM diagnosis codes listed in the policy. Furthermore, some services have such a wide variety of conditions that all possible codes are not listed. These services would be denied under certain circumstances, which may or may not be clearly indicated in the policy (Scichilone 2002, p. 48). Also, LMRPs may be revised, but the software may not be immediately updated.

This software should be used with caution. It is inappropriate to rely solely on software applications to provide the appropriate information to substantiate medical necessity for items and services ordered. Software programs only create an efficient way to manage LMRPs; they cannot substitute for familiarity with the entire LMRP and review of the health record documentation to validate medical necessity. (Scichilone 2002, p. 48). Medical necessity screening software is best employed after a coding expert has coded the diagnostic information provided by the ordering physician or practitioner. For example, is the software going to be able to recognize that a diagnosis of "history of venous thrombosis" means a past history, not a current condition? Will it know what to do with a "rule out" diagnosis?

The risk of reliance on screening software has some pitfalls that should be recognized before investment. When the software to screen for medical necessity is used **prior to the service:**

- ABNs may be issued by the hospital when the service does not appear to be medically necessary, though the documentation in the record kept by the ordering physician supports coverage. Medicare beneficiaries may end up believing they must pay out of pocket for services that should be covered when a claim is filed. Also, it is possible that a covered diagnosis code may be assigned by the hospital coding staff based on information confirmed by a physician following the test results, when prior to the test, the clinician did not have enough information to report a diagnosis on the covered list. Medicare would pay for the service claimed and there would be no need to bill the patient, even though the patient was told up front that Medicare might not pay for the service.

- When the software rejects the service as not medically necessary, the patient has to decide whether to pay for the test themselves or ask the provider to submit a claim for the purpose of getting a denial. Faced with these choices, patients may elect not to get a service their physician believes is needed. This situation can be complicated by the fact that when this occurs in a hospital, the physician is usually not available to speak with the patient and explain why the service was ordered. If the hospital indicates that it will go back to the physician for a "better" diagnosis, questions may be raised about the ethics of the coding process.

- Valuable time and resources are wasted selecting an "acceptable" diagnosis from the physician to progress with the service rejected by the software screening, even though the diagnosis provided would be appropriate and necessary for the condition, despite not being listed in an LMRP table.

When the software is used on the back end of the process **before a claim is filed:**

- Some providers using screening software might elect not to file a claim for a questionable or non-covered service and will write off the costs rather than submit a claim to the fiscal intermediary (FI) for the denial. If this is routine, there are instances where hospitals are losing dollars that they deserve and not taking advantage of the appeal process to [effect] coverage changes. They are also increasing the risk of providing inappropriate incentives for patient services by waiving patient coinsurance and deductibles and providing free care. For questionable services involving medical necessity, a claim must be filed to determine coverage requirements for the beneficiary. According to the Medicare Hospital Manual, Pub. 10, Section 430, these are the only circumstances where a provider should not submit a claim to Medicare:

  —The patient is not enrolled under Part B.

  —It is obvious that only noncovered services have been rendered.

  —Payment was made in full by the National Institutes of Health Grant, Public Health Service, Veterans Administration (VA), or other governmental entity, or liability insurance.

  —The period was covered in full by workers' compensation (including Beneficiary Liability), automobile medical, no-fault insurance, or in the situations described in [sections] 471E and 472E for an employer group health plan or large group health plan when you know that the individual has already met his deductible.

- The "back door" approach [ensures] that patients get the services the physician ordered without delay or questions but increases compliance risks by encouraging the search for a "payable code." This can also cause the hospital to lose money by providing services that will be denied because they are not covered, and then cannot be billed to the patient because no ABN was completed at the time of service.

- When a service is rejected with the code provided, the hospital may try to find a covered code using inappropriate methods such as assumptive coding, creation of leading inquiries to physicians, or using a source document for a code not appropriate for that encounter (such as documentation from a previous encounter). All of these practices are ethically questionable and increase the likelihood of false claims allegations against the hospital. Software tools should never be used as a reason to change or manipulate a patient's diagnosis for claims reporting without full knowledge and consent of the physician and assurance that clinical documentation supports the actual condition reported (Scichilone 2002, pp. 48, 50).

Organizations should research medical necessity screening software carefully and seek feedback from other organizations using the same software prior to purchasing it. It can serve as a useful tool, but should not be used to completely replace human review. Educated and ethical coding practices should continue to form the cornerstone of the billing process.

Managing Medical Necessity Requirements

The following are some tips for achieving compliance with payers' medical necessity requirements:

- **Report the patient's actual condition** that reflects the reason for the test. If a hospital allows ordering physicians to submit the diagnosis codes rather than the narrative description of the reason for service, there is a risk that the code is not fully accurate when compared to the source document. Further, the narrative description enables the technician carrying out [the test] to understand the indications for the service and not have to translate the numeric code back to clinical information.

- **Use a requisition form** that documents the reason for the service and enforce its use. Then, a coding professional specifically trained in coding conventions and reimbursement requirements can translate the information into ICD-9-CM codes used on the claim form.

- **Make sure** clinical documentation forms or formats **prompt** the users to fully document medical necessity for services ordered.

- When ABNs are required, they are best **administered by the ordering physician** so that the patient is fully informed of the implications of payment or declining the service. This is much harder to accomplish at the hospital. Software assistance is most useful at this stage to educate physicians concerning Medicare coverage requirements and policies. For complete information about giving Medicare beneficiaries appropriate notification go to www.hcfa.gov/medicare/BNI.

- Audit claims with medical necessity denials and **look for patterns** by actual service or by ordering physician. When trends are identified, targeted education can help improve documentation or communication of the reason for services to minimize denials and rejections for covered services. This education can ensure that noncovered services are identified in time to get the required notices given and allow the patient to make a fully informed choice.

- **Use software as a tool** for managing coverage requirements and providing readily available education. Avoid reliance on any product that suggests codes when the conditions cannot be fully supported in documentation. Also, confirm that the product is using the correct set of guidelines. For hospitals, those are the policies that apply to institutions submitting claims to FIs. There are currently differences by locality and also between FIs and carriers for the same service, so make sure the tool you are using applies the correct set of guidelines to the reported services.

- **Ask** the software vendor to illustrate how the software will help your facility manage those services where discrete code sets are not available or all-inclusive and the policy relies on text descriptions rather than ICD-9-CM code lists.

- **Be confident** that when accurate clinical data is translated into the appropriate clinical codes the correct coverage decision will result with or without software assistance. When it doesn't, be sure to exercise the right to appeal (Scichilone 2002, p. 50).

The healthcare organization's compliance program should include processes for ensuring that medical necessity criteria are checked prior to performing the test and that the test was ordered by a physician or other appropriately licensed individual. If feasible, assigning a coding professional to the registration area helps to ensure the accuracy of the process for verifying that medical necessity requirements have been met. In addition to the importance of correct assignment of the diagnosis codes, it is also important to identify the correct procedure code so that the applicable LMRP will be utilized for determining medical necessity. Of course, it is probably unrealistic for an organization to be able to staff the registration area with coding personnel twenty-four hours a day, but certainly providing coding staff during the time when most of the diagnostic outpatient services are being performed would address the majority of the medical necessity issues.

The best approach to ensure compliance with medical necessity requirements is complete and accurate diagnostic information provided by the ordering physician or practitioner at the time a test is ordered. The key to achieving this is thorough, ongoing education of the medical staff on medical necessity requirements and the importance of providing complete, accurate diagnoses describing the reason(s) test(s) are being ordered, supported by the documentation in their office health records. The organization performing the diagnostic tests should regularly educate physicians on the medical necessity definitions and rules of the various payers it does business with. Physicians should be educated on the reasons why they are required to provide diagnostic information when ordering tests. Examples include the following:

- The Medicare requirement that services are reasonable and necessary for diagnosis and treatment

- The development of LMRPs containing diagnoses that support Medicare's definition of medical necessity

- The inability for the provider furnishing the test to be reimbursed unless a diagnosis supporting the medical necessity of the test is submitted on the claim or an ABN has been issued to the patient

- The possibility that the Medicare contractor will request a copy of the physician's office record if insufficient or nonsupportive diagnostic information is submitted on the claim

Educational programs should emphasize that the diagnostic information provided on the requisition must accurately reflect the patient's condition and be supported by documentation in the physician's office record. It is *never* appropriate to simply select a payable diagnosis in order to ensure that the test will be reimbursed by Medicare.

It is unethical and fraudulent to report a diagnosis code on the claim that is not supported by health record documentation simply because it is "payable." If the service does not meet the payer's medical necessity standards, the patient should be informed of the likelihood of the service being denied prior to furnishing the service, and, in the case of Medicare, an ABN should be issued. The patient should be allowed the option of choosing to forego the test. If the patient decides not to have the test, the ordering physician or practitioner should be notified.

For healthcare settings other than outpatient facilities or physicians' offices, the applicable medical necessity requirements should be reviewed and appropriate processes put in place to ensure compliance. For example, in the home health setting, the plan of care must be certified by a physician who is a doctor of medicine, osteopathy, or podiatric medicine. Periodic clinical reviews, both prior and subsequent to billing for services, should be conducted to verify that patients are receiving only medically necessary services. Home health agencies should examine the frequency and duration of the services they perform to determine, in consultation with a physician, whether the patient's medical condition justifies the number of visits provided and billed. Policies and procedures should be implemented to verify that beneficiaries have actually received the appropriate level and number of services billed. The importance of accurately documenting the services performed and billed should be stressed to caregivers. Confirmation that services were provided as claimed could be obtained by periodically contacting (via e-mail, telephone, or in person) a random sample of patients and interviewing the clinical staff involved. Home health agencies need to establish processes to ensure that physician orders are received and properly documented prior to billing for services. A leading reason for home health claims denials is failure to obtain physician orders in a timely manner.

Arrangements with Consultants

While the utilization of a coding consultant can be helpful in identifying and resolving errors and improving coding accuracy, reliance on improper advice from a consultant substantially increases an organization's risk of sanctions and/or fines. Therefore, it is imperative for an organization to select a consultant carefully. The Department of Health and Human Services (HHS) Office of Inspector General (OIG) released a Special Advisory Bulletin in June 2001 regarding certain consulting practices. The bulletin addressed the following questionable practices that have been identified in healthcare consulting:

- **[Making] Illegal or misleading representations:** Some consultants have made claims that they have "special" relationships with the CMS or the OIG, including statements that they are "endorsed" by one of these agencies. Neither of these agencies endorses consulting companies.

- **[Making] Promises and guarantees:** Consultants may make financial promises or guarantees that cannot be met. This may include a promise that consulting services will result in a certain dollar or percentage increase in reimbursement. The practices used to keep these promises may be fraudulent.

- **Encouraging abusive practices:** Healthcare consulting companies may educate providers to use inappropriate codes to increase reimbursement or to misinterpret coding rules and regulations to maximize reimbursement. The provider may not question the vendor and, in fact, trust the information provided as part of the vendor education.

- **Discouraging compliance efforts:** Certain consultants discourage certain compliance efforts, such as coding compliance reviews. Compliance reviews are a recommended component of the OIG's Compliance Guidance. Should problems remain undetected, the provider may be at risk for potential fraud and abuse violations (Hammen 2001, p. 26).

According to the advisory bulletin (OIG 2001b, p. 2):

Responsible consultants play an integral role in developing and maintaining practices that enhance a client's business objectives, as well as in improving the overall integrity of the health care system. [The OIG] believes that most consultants, like most providers, are honest, and that the vast majority of relationships between providers and consultants are legitimate business activities.

Unfortunately, a small minority of unscrupulous consultants engage in improper practices or encourage abuse of the Medicare and Medicaid programs. Depending on the circumstances, these practices may expose both the consultants and their clients to potential legal liability. Hiring a consultant does not relieve a provider of responsibility for ensuring the integrity of its dealings with the Federal health care programs.

A report issued by the General Accounting Office (GAO) in June 2001, titled Health Care: Consultants' Billing Advice May Lead to Improperly Paid Insurance Claims,

provided instances of inappropriate or fraudulent advice given by a consulting company. This advice could result in violations of both civil and criminal statutes. During the course of the education, advice was provided regarding:

- Avoidance of reporting and refunding overpayments

- Creation of documentation to support higher level evaluation and management (E/M) code assignments when a lower level code is appropriate

- Limitation of services to Medicaid patients to avoid the lower payments usually associated with Medicaid

The GAO suggested to the OIG that workshops and seminars should be monitored to identify advice that could result in improper or excessive claims for reimbursement.

Healthcare providers need to be vigilant and exercise prudence when selecting and relying on consultants (Hammen 2001, p. 26)

The following criteria can assist providers in selecting external coding consulting companies. A potential vendor should meet the following criteria:

- **Follows the Cooperating Parties'** (AHIMA, American Hospital Association, CMS, and National Center for Health Statistics) **official ICD-9-CM guidelines for coding and reporting.** These guidelines have been approved for use in coding Medicare, Medicaid, and CHAMPUS claims. You may want to review the vendor's internal coding guidelines to ensure consistency with the official coding guidelines. Additionally, if a physician coding quality review is conducted, the vendor should be well versed in the application of E/M documentation guidelines that have been approved by CMS in assigning the appropriate level of CPT evaluation and management codes.

- **Reports overcoding, undercoding, and coding quality errors that do not affect reimbursement.** The primary goals should be to assess and improve coding accuracy. High-quality coded data depends on complete and accurate coding that reflects the documented diagnoses and procedures. The provider can then be assured that the billing is accurate and that its healthcare statistics will provide an accurate view of the case mix for determining future services, managed care contracting, and profiling.

- **Charges fixed fees instead of contingency fees.** The OIG compliance program guidance advises that compensation for billing consultants should not provide any financial incentive to improperly upcode claims. By charging the healthcare provider a fixed fee for coding quality reviews rather than a percentage of the money "found," the incentive for upcoding is eliminated.

- **Employs only AHIMA-credentialed coding staff** and is willing to provide proof of the credential status of each employee providing services. Attainment of an AHIMA credential indicate that the individual has met AHIMA competencies for the particular credential and participates in ongoing continuing education.

- **Justifies recommendations for changes to coding or DRG assignment through the use of appropriate references.** Appropriate references would include the use of the official coding guidelines, E/M documentation guidelines, *Coding Clinic for ICD-9-CM,* or *CPT Assistant.* If the consultant cannot justify a recommended change, the healthcare provider may want to contact an official source (the Central Office on ICD-9-CM for ICD-9-CM questions or the American Medical Association for CPT questions) prior to agreeing with the consultant's recommendation.

- **Educates consulting staff on consistent application of official coding guidelines.** The vendor should be able to produce documentation indicating the provision of at least annual or semi-annual educational programs for its consulting staff. This may represent an educational session developed and presented by the company itself or sending the consulting staff to external programs.

- **Has its own compliance program and will provide you with a copy.** If a coding compliance vendor does not have a compliance program in place, how can it assist you in ensuring your compliance? Their program should be verified for consistency with your organization's compliance program. The coding philosophy of the selected vendor should reflect your organization's philosophy in ensuring complete and accurate coding. In any case, the firm's representative should be asked to sign an agreement that any personnel assigned to the healthcare organization will abide by the elements of its compliance program.

- **Monitors the quality of work performed by its consulting staff and institutes corrective action to address unacceptable levels of coding accuracy.** The vendor should be able to provide assurance that its work meets certain quality standards.

- **Educates provider staff as a component of its services.** A good external coding quality review should include education related to findings of upcoding, undercoding, and data quality as a component of its services. Education should be provided for both the coding staff and the physicians in order to address findings related to coding quality and documentation. Technical or clinical education related to trends identified during the audit process should be included in the educational component.

- **Has never been convicted of fraudulent practices.** In keeping with the regulations for providers in the Balanced Budget Act of 1997, vendors who have been convicted of fraudulent practices should be avoided. It is in the best interest of the healthcare provider to ensure that they are receiving high-quality, ethical services.

- **Provides services under attorney-client privilege.** When an attorney representing a provider requests auditing services under attorney-client privilege, the vendor will work with and report only to the attorney. There will be no communication between the vendor and the healthcare provider. This protects the results of the coding compliance audit from future "discovery."

- **Has credible client references.** Don't settle for a prepared list of references—this list will only give you the names of individuals with which the vendor wants you to speak. Request a list of and contact the five clients most recently served by the vendor. Ensure that they were satisfied with the coding philosophy of the vendor, the fees, and the quality of service (Hammen 2001, pp. 26, 28, 30).

Before signing a contract for coding consulting services, the qualifications of the firm providing the services should be evaluated carefully. The following questions offer some guidance:

- What is the background of the firm's management staff?

- What experience and qualifications do its personnel have?

- What are the firm's continuing education requirements for its staff?

- What mechanisms does the firm have in place to monitor the quality of its work? How is quality measured? What are its accuracy standards?

- Does the firm have a corporate compliance program? If so, is it consistent with the healthcare organization's compliance program?

- How is the firm reimbursed for services (flat fee, hourly rate, per record rate, contingency based)?

The references and specific qualifications of the individuals responsible for conducting the work at the healthcare organization should be checked thoroughly. Do they possess an HIM credential? Does their experience match the type of work they will be doing? For example, does the person performing DRG validation have inpatient coding experience in a prospective payment system (PPS) hospital, or does the individual reviewing a physician's E/M services have experience with this type of coding? Organizations should contact the most recent clients served by the consultant to determine the quality of the work performed and the level of satisfaction with the services provided.

The organization's policies and procedures should stipulate that it has the right to refuse to implement a consultant's recommendation when it can demonstrate that the consultant's advice conflicts with official coding guidelines or regulatory requirements. For every recommendation accepted that is contingent upon additional physician documentation, the physician should incorporate the documentation in the health record before submitting the claim containing the revised codes (or, if it is a retrospective review, before resubmitting a claim or submitting a DRG adjustment request).

A healthcare provider can protect itself from investigation by ensuring that the coding consulting company selected provides high-quality, ethical services and adheres to all applicable federal and state laws and regulations. As the OIG notes in the conclusion of its advisory bulletin, "if a consultant's advice seems to be too good to be true, it probably is."

Retention of Records

Written policies and procedures should be established to address the creation, distribution, retention, storage, retrieval, and destruction of all types of documents. Types of documents include health records, claims documents, and compliance documents. Health record and claims documentation should be retained according to applicable federal and state law and regulations.

All organizations should develop and implement a system for maintaining all records necessary to demonstrate the integrity of the compliance process and confirm the effectiveness of the program. Documents include the following types:

- Employee certifications relating to the code of conduct, training, and other compliance initiatives

- Copies of compliance training materials

- Results of auditing/monitoring activities, including corrective action plans and follow-up

- Reports of investigations

- Outcomes

- Disciplinary actions taken

- Relevant correspondence with carriers, fiscal intermediaries, private health insurers, CMS, and state survey and certification agencies

The organization's legal counsel should be consulted regarding the retention of compliance records (such as employee training documentation, reports from the hotline, results of internal investigations, and results of auditing and monitoring). These records must be maintained for a sufficient length of time to ensure their availability to prove compliance with laws and regulations, if needed.

Health records must be secured against loss, destruction, unauthorized access, unauthorized reproduction, corruption, and damage. All health record documentation should be secured in a safe place and access should be limited to avoid accidental or intentional fabrication, alteration, or destruction of records.

Policies and procedures should be developed to ensure the integrity of the information maintained by the organization and to ensure that records can be easily located and accessed within a well-organized filing or alternative retrieval system. There should be a back-up system to ensure the integrity of data, and policies should provide for a regular system back-up to ensure that no information is lost.

When seeking advice from a representative of a federal healthcare program or other payer, a record of the request and any written or oral response (or nonresponse) should be retained in order to support any actions taken or policies and/or procedures developed as a result of the advice received.

Confidentiality

Policies and procedures ensuring the confidentiality and privacy of financial, medical, personnel, and other sensitive information should be developed, implemented, audited, and enforced. Policies and procedures should address both electronic and hard copy documents. Policies and procedures related to privacy of medical information should be developed and/or updated to ensure compliance with the HIPAA privacy regulations.

Compliance as an Element of Performance Review

Organizational policy should stipulate that the promotion of, and adherence to, the elements of the compliance program is a factor in the performance review of managers and supervisors. Managers and supervisors of the coding process have a duty to discuss compliance policies, official coding guidelines, and regulatory requirements affecting the coding process with all coding staff. If the organization outsources part or all of the coding function, managers and supervisors should ensure that the outsourced staff are made aware of these requirements.

Managers and supervisors should inform coding staff that strict compliance with these policies and requirements is a condition of employment. In the case of outsourced staff, the company employing the coding professionals should be informed that compliance by its personnel is a condition of the contractual arrangement and that violations will be cause for termination of the contract. Managers and supervisors also should explain to their personnel the consequences (that is, disciplinary action) of violating policies and regulatory requirements. Fulfillment of these managerial responsibilities should be a factor in managers' and supervisors' performance evaluations.

Training and Education

The proper education and training of managers, supervisors, employees, physicians, and independent contractors and the continuous retraining of current personnel at every level are important elements of any effective compliance program. Participation in training programs should be made a condition of continued employment, and failure to comply should result in disciplinary action, including possible termination. Moreover, participation in training programs should be a factor in performance evaluations.

Qualifications for Coding Positions

It is highly recommended that anyone being considered for a coding position receive formal coding education prior to assuming the position. Every healthcare organization should maintain job descriptions that outline each position's necessary qualifications and responsibilities. Positions with responsibility for coding, even if coding is only a small portion of the individual's job, should be filled with individuals who have the appropriate educational background and training. Using unqualified staff could pose compliance risks for an organization.

Qualifications for coding include formal training in the following areas:

- Anatomy and physiology
- Medical terminology
- Pathology and disease processes
- Pharmacology
- Health record format and content
- Reimbursement methodologies
- Conventions, rules, and guidelines for current classification systems (for example, ICD-9-CM and CPT)

Additionally, coding professionals must be able to apply the competencies AHIMA has identified for inpatient and ambulatory coding. These competencies can be found in the candidate handbooks for the AHIMA coding certification exams, which are available on the AHIMA Web site at the following addresses:

- For registered health information administrators and technicians: www.ahima.org/certification/rhia.rhit.guide.pdf
- For certified coding specialists and physician-based specialists: www.ahima.org/certification/ccs.ccsp.guide.pdf
- For certified coding associates: www.ahima.org/certification/exam.html

Coding education can be obtained from a range of sources and through various means. AHIMA offers Internet-based basic, intermediate, and advanced coding education. Many community colleges offer coding and/or HIM programs that incorporate coding courses. Accreditation by AHIMA signifies that the program has met AHIMA's standards and utilizes AHIMA's model coding curriculum. AHIMA's approval criteria for coding certificate programs ensure that students receive the fundamental knowledge to meet basic coding competency standards. Approval criteria for coding certificate programs identify those specialized programs that meet standards of educational quality. To receive approval from AHIMA, organizations offering coding instruction (academic institutions, healthcare organizations, private companies, and others) must demonstrate sufficient compliance to the outlined criteria, which include the following:

- Instruction incorporates AHIMA coding curriculum knowledge clusters

  —Biomedical sciences

  —Information technology

  —Healthcare data content and structure

  —Healthcare delivery system

  —Clinical classification systems

  —Reimbursement methodology

  —Professional practice experience, practicum, and/or internship

- Appropriate educational systems/policies and published materials

- Adequate program leadership, management and faculty/developers knowledge base

- Appropriate learning experiences to develop required competencies

A copy of AHIMA's Coding Program Curriculum Guide can be obtained by contacting AHIMA.

A job candidate's coding skills may be assessed in a number of ways, and the organization may choose to adopt one or a combination of approaches. For example, a coding assessment may be developed and administered. If this is the approach chosen, the test should meet the Equal Employment Opportunity Commission (EEOC) guidelines. Working with the organization's human resources department will help ensure compliance with the EEOC guidelines. (More information about the EEOC can be obtained at www.eeoc.gov.) The organization must be able to demonstrate that the test reflects performance required on the job. The test must fairly reflect the type of coding required for the job and the typical types of cases coded in the healthcare organization. For example, an inpatient coding test should not be given to someone applying for an outpatient coding job. The coding test and the required passing score should be the same for all candidates for a particular position.

Successful attainment of a national coding certification is another way to determine coding competency. In addition to the general HIM credentials—registered health information technician (RHIT) and registered health information administrator (RHIA)—

AHIMA also offers several specialized coding certifications: certified coding associate (CCA), certified coding specialist (CCS), and certified coding specialist–physician-based (CCS-P). The RHIA, RHIT, and CCA credentials all denote entry-level competency. The RHIA and RHIT credentials denote entry-level competency in multiple aspects of health information practice, including coding, whereas the CCA credential denotes entry-level competency in coding alone. The CCS and CCS-P credentials signify mastery-level coding proficiency gained through experience or additional education beyond basic competency. The coding certification obtained should match the skills sought or required for the position in question. For example, possession of AHIMA's CCS-P credential does not demonstrate competency as an inpatient coding professional. The CCA credential may be appropriate for registration personnel or other access positions where a basic level of coding knowledge is important.

Extensive coding experience, with excellent references verifying coding expertise, may be considered sufficient evidence of an individual's coding qualifications. However, the individual's coding experience must match the type of coding required by the position for which he or she is applying. If the individual's past coding experience is only in ambulatory care and he or she is applying for an inpatient coding position, it may be necessary to administer a coding skill assessment test or to look to coding certification as a way to verify his or her inpatient coding skills. AHIMA's Internet-based Coding Assessment and Training Solutions program (www.ahimacampus.org) offers tools for assessing coding skills and identifying specific areas requiring improvement.

If the healthcare organization is considering hiring a graduate of a coding certificate program and he or she does not possess other qualifications (such as nationally recognized coding credentials or extensive experience), the organization should check the program's accreditation status with AHIMA. If it has not been approved by AHIMA, the program's curriculum, content, and instructor qualifications should be reviewed carefully for appropriateness. It is insufficient to review only a curriculum outline. Although course names may be appropriate, course content may not. For example, the program may include a course on ICD-9-CM coding, but if the students learn nothing about the official coding guidelines, the course is unacceptable. Quality coding educational programs utilize AHIMA's model coding curriculum. Organizations may want to consider only accepting graduates from coding programs that have been approved by AHIMA.

Successful completion of an HIM educational or coding certificate program does not, in itself, establish the advanced-level coding competency necessary for many coding positions in a complex regulatory environment. Completion of an HIM or coding program, and successful attainment of the RHIA, RHIT, or CCA credentials, signifies only that an individual has met entry-level skill requirements. In the absence of requisite coding experience, the work of these entry-level professionals should be closely monitored until they have demonstrated that they are able to consistently meet the organization's quality standards.

Continuing Education and Ongoing Training

All employees of the HIM department should receive annual training on the basic features of the compliance program so that they understand what compliance is, its importance, their role in maintaining compliance through application of standards, and their obligation to report any potential violations according to the organization's policy. Additionally, employees should be educated on the various mechanisms available to them for reporting potential violations. The organization's disciplinary policy for various types of violations should be included in the educational program that all employees attend. All HIM staff involved in coding should receive extensive ongoing coding education.

All newly hired coding professionals should receive extensive training on the organization's HIM compliance program. Key components of the program, such as the code of conduct, should be communicated to newly hired employees prior to beginning their job responsibilities. New coders should receive extensive training in the organization's coding policies and procedures. Random reviews of their coding should be conducted to ensure comprehension of and adherence to the organization's compliance program and policies and procedures. The coding reviews of newly hired employees with advanced-level competency (that is, extensive qualifications and/or experience) may be less intensive than that of entry-level personnel but more intensive than that of seasoned departmental staff. For example, since attainment of AHIMA's CCS and CCS-P credentials signify mastery-level coding proficiency, an organization may decide that newly-hired staff with these credentials require less rigorous monitoring. Such a decision would be based on the past experience of the individuals holding these credentials.

All entry-level coding professionals should be closely monitored and supervised until their ability to code accurately (in a variety of situations), to make appropriate decisions (for example, determining when physician clarification is needed), and to apply multiple-payer regulations and policies has been ensured (the time frame will vary according to individual skills and learning curves). Current coding staff can serve as mentors and trainers for new coding professionals. Employees, physicians, and independent contractors should be required to have a minimum number of educational hours per year with the number of required hours varying for different categories of individuals. For example, coding staff should be required to have a higher number of educational hours than file clerks or record processing staff. Education can consist of the following:

- In-house programs by internal staff or consultants

- Seminars at an outside organization, including both face-to-face seminars and those using technological media such as audio conferencing, satellite conferences, or Internet-based training

- Self-study instruction such as correspondence courses, videotapes, audio tapes, and software programs

- Self-assessments such as continuing education quizzes for reading journal articles

Utilization of a variety of training methods is preferred to meet all learning styles.

Computer-based training can be particularly advantageous because it improves the quality and consistency of the training (both the content and the delivery are more consistent), enhances the ability to target training, lowers training costs over the long term, and generally incorporates mechanisms to administer and measure the effectiveness of training efforts. Computer-based training is self-paced, more conducive to individual schedules, more readily accessible, quickly updated in comparison to other types of training programs, and immediately accessed. AHIMA offers Internet-based training to enhance coding skills and other HIM skill areas. (More information is available at www.ahimacampus.org.)

Regular meetings of the coding staff should be conducted to discuss difficult cases, individual questions, new or revised guidelines or regulations, and new diseases being treated or new technologies being utilized. Meeting frequency depends on the size of the organization and the number of coding professionals. Focused coding training programs should be developed in response to areas of deficiency identified during monitoring or auditing and as new regulatory or guideline changes occur (that is, in October for ICD-9-CM updates and in January for CPT/HCPCS updates). Education on identified coding errors should always be provided to the coding staff, regardless of whether the errors caused accuracy rates to fall below the standard.

The coding staff should receive training not only on the coding process but also on interpretation of physician documentation and techniques for communicating with physicians (for example, how to query the physician for clarification regarding a documentation or coding issue). Techniques for effectively communicating with physicians and how to interpret documentation should be included in the topics for educational programs. An effective training method might be to ask the coding staff to research coding issues and discuss their findings at a future meeting.

HIM coding staff, physicians, other healthcare professionals, and appropriate billing and ancillary department staff (such as utilization review personnel and those individuals involved in chargemaster maintenance) should receive training on the HIM compliance program on an annual basis. The training should include, as appropriate for the target audience, acceptable documentation practices (including the prohibition against altering health records); accurate coding practices; and regulatory requirements pertaining to coding, billing, and documentation. Part of the compliance program education should stress that manipulation, fabrication, alteration, or omission of information in an effort to falsely support medical necessity or affect health plan coverage is a compliance violation. Staff and clinicians should be encouraged to suggest ways to improve coding accuracy and documentation practices such as by employing additional resources or revised processes. Healthcare professionals need to understand the effect documentation has on the clinical, operational, and financial aspects of healthcare delivery. (See appendix C for a list of suggested educational topics for non-HIM personnel.)

Various disciplines within the healthcare organization can participate in educating each other. For example, HIM staff can educate ancillary departments on the importance of documentation to support medical necessity of ordered tests and the need for annual updating of the chargemaster. HIM staff can also educate physicians and other departments' staff on coding, reimbursement, and documentation requirements as well as fraud and abuse issues. Physicians can educate coding personnel on new surgical or diagnostic procedures and techniques and various clinical disease processes. Coding staff should prepare questions related to the clinical topic in advance, which will help the presenter know what to cover and will improve both the coding professionals' and clinicians' understanding of the relationship between documentation and coding. Physicians' office staff should be invited to attend hospital in-house training programs. These opportunities for office and hospital staff to learn from each other will foster communication and collaboration.

The medical staff should receive education on documentation requirements and the relationship of documentation to coding. When documentation deficiencies are identified, focused training programs should be provided and may consist of one-on-one training.

Examples of documentation problems that may need to be addressed in training programs for physicians include the following:

- Inconsistent health record documentation

- Incomplete progress notes

- Undocumented care

- Test results not being addressed in the physician documentation

- Historical diagnoses being documented as current diagnoses

- Longstanding, chronic conditions that are not being documented at all

It is best to use actual examples of documentation problems during the educational programs to demonstrate how poor documentation results in inaccurate coding and reimbursement. Physician educational programs held for short periods of time (for example, thirty to forty-five minutes) tend to fit better into physicians' daily schedules. Planning programs focused exclusively on compliance issues is also better than discussing these issues in a meeting with a larger agenda. Sandwiching presentations in this way may cause compliance issues to be overshadowed. Inhouse newsletters serve as an excellent method in which to augment and reinforce the material presented during educational programs. Attendance should be mandatory for all employees including physicians, and disciplinary action should be taken for lack of participation. Since physicians are best influenced by peers, seeking an advocate on the medical staff who help promote the importance of complete and accurate documentation thereby bridging the gap between ethical coding practices and clinical documentation. Penalties such as fines and imprisonment should be avoided as a way to motivate physicians. Instead, an organization should stress that improved efficiency and better patient care can result from effective documentation practices.

The compliance officer should be involved in the design of educational programs for physicians. This involvement will ensure the programs are designed appropriately such that there is no appearance of inducing referrals through the provision of free services to the physicians. Allied health personnel (therapists, pharmacists, and nurses) can educate coding staff on clinical issues pertaining to their respective disciplines. HIM staff can educate billing staff on the coding process. In turn, billing staff can educate HIM staff on the billing process and guidelines, including claims rejections and appeals. The healthcare organization might consider conducting periodic joint education programs for coding and billing staff. Such programs could address the relationship between coding and billing, the coding systems and reporting guidelines, how to communicate with payers, the importance of coding when claims are denied or delayed, and discussion of the organization's risk areas. The importance of involving coding staff in the resolution of claims denials related to coding issues and the potentially serious consequences of codes being changed on a claim without involvement of the coding staff also can be addressed.

Proactive cooperation and collaboration can prevent many inappropriate practices and inaccurate claims submissions from occurring. Registration personnel should be properly trained on the compliance impact of diagnostic and other clinical information that they obtain during the registration process. All of the employees involved in the reimbursement process, including registrars, coding professionals, schedulers, physicians, accounting personnel, case management staff, utilization review staff, quality assurance staff, ancillary clinical departments (such as laboratory, radiology), and data entry clerks should be brought together. Staff can gain exposure to other, related functions that make up the big picture through email newsletters and small interdepartmental group discussions and interactions.

Training (especially training on new or significantly modified regulations, guidelines, or codes) should be personal and interactive. Through discussion of new requirements and the use of case scenarios to show their proper application, a thorough understanding of the requirements can be demonstrated. Interactive discussions of the latest issues of *Coding Clinic for ICD-9-CM* and *CPT Assistant* can help to ensure comprehension of the content of these publications. If the healthcare organization has evening, weekend, part-time, or as needed (also known as prn) staff, it should consider ways to include these individuals in its training programs. Nursing facilities should provide focused training on MDS completion and proper health record documentation to support the MDS.

All independent contractors and other external agents involved in the coding or reimbursement processes (such as consultants or contracted coding or billing services) should receive training on the organization's HIM compliance program. In addition, they should be asked to sign an agreement to abide by the organization's program as part of the terms of their contract.

If the organization has both contract and employed coding professionals, the contract coding professionals should be required to have at least as much training and experience as the employed coding professionals. In addition to receiving training on the organization's coding policies and procedures, the contract coding professionals' work should be reviewed for accuracy and the contract coding professionals should be expected to maintain the same accuracy standards as the employed coding professionals.

The individual responsible for overseeing the HIM compliance program should maintain attendance rosters for all training programs, as well as copies of agendas and handouts. Sign-in sheets, rather than pretyped rosters, should be used to verify attendance, and attendees should be asked to sign in at the conclusion of the program. In addition, on either the sign-in sheet or a separate document, employees should be sign an acknowledgment of their comprehension of the material presented during the program. For attendance at seminars outside the organization, participants should be asked to provide a copy of the continuing education certificate (or other document verifying attendance), agenda, and handouts. These records should be made available to the corporate compliance officer upon request.

It is important to assess the effectiveness of training, such as the level of comprehension of the material presented and the effectiveness of the delivery and media utilized. The effectiveness of educational programs depends on establishing well-defined objectives for the program, creating a test instrument based on these objectives, and providing follow-up and appropriate corrective actions to address unacceptable test results. An objective should be developed for each specific competency that is expected to be gleaned from the program. Designing test questions around each objective will ensure that the organization is following through on the intended purpose of the program. Maintain documentation of all test results. Documentation of employees who have achieved acceptable scores on the test provides the organization with proof that the employee received the education and understood and internalized the concepts.

Continuous and immediate follow-up should be provided to those employees with unacceptable test scores. This follow-up should consist of retraining and retesting. Failure to obtain an acceptable score on a pre-established number of retests should result in disciplinary action. In its program guidances, the OIG states that one way to assess the knowledge, awareness, and perceptions of an organization's employees is through the use of a validated survey instrument. This can be accomplished through employee questionnaires, interviews, or focus groups. If the survey process indicates that participants didn't get the intended message, the approach to training should be modified until the expected results are achieved. Program evaluations are also useful feedback tools. Because different people learn best in different ways, the best approach is to vary the manner of delivery to sustain people's interest and also ensure they get the message.

Organizational policies should require that coding staff meet the organization's established qualifications, continually improve their skills, and keep up-to-date on pertinent regulations and coding practice standards. Job descriptions and educational requirements should be regularly reviewed and updated.

Communication

An established mechanism for employees to report perceived compliance violations must be in place. Organizations must be able to demonstrate that all reports of perceived violations are promptly investigated and that, when necessary, appropriate corrective action is taken. The organization's lines of communication and reporting protocol for compliance-related issues should be clearly communicated to all employees. For example, the organization may wish to stipulate the types of issues to be reported to the employee's supervisor rather than directly to the HIM compliance specialist or corporate compliance officer. However, employees should be encouraged to report any issue to the HIM compliance specialist or corporate compliance officer that they either do not feel comfortable reporting to a supervisor or do not feel the supervisor has adequately investigated and addressed. Although every effort should be made to educate employees on what a compliance-related issue is and the purpose of the organization's compliance reporting protocol, employees should not be chastised when they report a concern to the wrong entity (for example, calling the corporate compliance officer with a human resources–related issue). Employees who feel they have been reprimanded for using the compliance-reporting protocol (regardless of the reason) will be less likely to report issues in the future, including true compliance issues.

In addition, an established mechanism should be in place for employees, physicians, and contractors to receive clarification on a policy or procedure, an element of the compliance program, or an answer to a billing or coding question. The defined process should specify a designated resource person to contact. Employee inquiries and the responses to them should be documented, dated, and maintained by the HIM compliance specialist or corporate compliance officer. Depending on the nature of the inquiry, it may be appropriate to share the clarification with other staff members. If several employees require clarification on the same issue, it may be necessary to revise the written policies and procedures to alleviate confusion.

Policies and procedures should address how a significant change in a regulation or guideline will be expeditiously communicated to all affected staff. Changes that significantly affect reimbursement may not be able to wait until the next scheduled coding professionals' meeting (unless the implementation date of the change is well after the meeting date).

All reporting mechanisms should take into consideration employees who work evenings or weekends when a supervisor, HIM compliance specialist, and corporate compliance officer may not be available. Moreover, a centralized source and systematic process for distributing information on healthcare statutes and regulations should be in place. It is imperative that coding staff be informed of all local, state, and federal regulations governing the coding of health data. Moreover, a mechanism should be in place to ensure that all affected staff are informed of payment policies, regulatory changes, new guidelines, and other important information. Therefore, if a provider bulletin or other official memorandum is received in one department, there also must be a process for its timely distribution outside that department. Communication to affected staff of updated regulations, standards, policies, or procedures should occur as soon as possible after the updated information becomes available and certainly before the effective date of the change. When a memo advising staff of a policy, procedure, or regulatory change is disseminated, the staff members should be asked to sign it, thereby acknowledging their receipt of the information. The memo, along with the staff signatures (and the date the staff read it), should be kept on file.

All documents containing regulatory information affecting coding should be maintained with the coding policies and procedures. Additionally, an established mechanism should be in place for communicating effectively with physicians on coding and documentation issues. If the organization has evening, weekend, part-time, or prn staff, it also should consider ways to expeditiously communicate important regulatory information to these staff members.

It is difficult to stay abreast of all of the new and updated regulatory information that comes out on a daily basis. However, the Internet has made it much easier to stay current. Organizations should consider subscribing to one of the free software programs that can monitor Web sites of interest and automatically notify you of any changes or updates. This eliminates the need to continually check the sites. Many government agencies also offer an email notification service that announces the release of new regulations, policies, or instructions. It is also helpful to stay in touch with colleagues. AHIMA's Communities of Practice (www.ahimanet.org) are an excellent way for AHIMA members to stay in touch with colleagues and get up-to-the-minute information concerning regulatory or legislative changes.

Auditing and Monitoring

An ongoing evaluation process is important to a successful compliance program. The process evaluates whether the standards, policies, and procedures are current and accurate, as well as whether there is compliance with them and appropriate submission of claims. If the standards, policies, or procedures are found to be ineffective or outdated, they require immediate updates. The auditing and monitoring of operations are key to ensuring compliance and adherence to government regulations, official coding rules and guidelines, and the healthcare organization's standards, policies, and procedures.

Monitoring is the ongoing internal review of operations conducted by an organization on a regular basis. *Auditing* is an infrequent, retrospective review usually conducted by an outside firm to ensure objectivity. Auditing is a more structured, formal reporting process than monitoring and is performed less frequently than monitoring. Auditing also tends to be focused on larger populations (Russo 1998).

An effective monitoring program allows an organization to detect and correct problems early, which minimizes the risk of civil financial penalties and administrative sanctions. Auditing and monitoring also identify areas of potential risk that may require closer attention and areas on which to focus additional education. Routine reviews help to ensure that errors and patterns of errors are identified and corrected early, before becoming major problems.

Internal organizational policy should identify the types of audits, reviews, and internal investigations, if any, that will be conducted under the direction of legal counsel so that attorney-client privilege regarding audit results is preserved, when appropriate.

Audit Design

A formalized audit process for compliance should be established by developing audit protocols. (See figure 3.) These should include policies and procedures for an audit process, periodic reporting, and corrective measures for identified problems. The audit process should be approached methodically with an organized plan that begins with a review of the areas of highest vulnerability (for example, DRGs targeted by the OIG or statistical variations from national norms). The following questions need to be addressed:

- What?
- Who?
- When and how often?
- What type of format?

Figure 3. **Factors to consider when designing an auditing/monitoring program**

- Objectives of the review
- Frequency of review
- Time period to be covered
- Record selection process (review population)
- Sample size and design
- Indicators
- Whether the review will be retrospective or prospective
- Data analysis techniques to be used
- Qualifications of personnel performing review
- Way in which results will be used to improve operations
- Report formats for tracking and analyzing audit results

The population to be reviewed might be all inpatients, all outpatients, all ambulatory surgery patients, all clinic patients, or all emergency department patients. Or the population might consist of a subset of one of these categories, such as Medicare inpatients only or Medicare inpatients with a diagnosis of pneumonia.

The scope of the review, frequency of reviews, and sample size depend on the size of the organization, available resources, number of coding professionals, prior identification of noncompliance, and the organization's known risk factors.

Indicators need to be defined. For example, types of indicators for a coding audit include the coding error rate, selection of principal diagnosis, accuracy of DRG assignment, and selection of discharge status. Indicators that measure performance in areas being scrutinized by the federal government should be developed (for example, frequently-upcoded DRGs). By analyzing multiple indicators, areas for further review can be prioritized. Once the indicators have been determined, the specifications for each indicator should be described. Specifications are instructions regarding what data elements are required and where each data element can be located (that is, the database where the data element can be found). An explicit description of the indicators allows consistent replication of the indicators so that results from audits performed at different times can be compared.

The use of statistical sampling (such as the OIG's RAT-STATS program) can help to serve as an early detection system of risk and vulnerabilities. In conjunction with investigation of identified problems and initiation of appropriate corrective action, statistical sampling can improve the effectiveness of the compliance program. Statistically valid sampling helps to limit the cost of labor resources necessary to carry out proactive auditing and monitoring.

Auditing and Monitoring of Coding and Documentation

Coding accuracy should be monitored through periodic reviews and regular monitoring. Periodically, a random sample of health records should be recoded to ensure that the coding was performed properly and the code assignments accurately reflect the services provided, as documented in the health records. Coding accuracy encompasses assignment of proper codes, appropriate code sequencing, and identification of all reportable diagnoses and procedures. Reviews of coding accuracy should include an assessment of the health record documentation to ensure that it is clear, complete, and accurately reflects the codes assigned. The scope of the review, frequency of reviews, and size of the sample depends on the size of the organization, available resources, the number of coding professionals, prior history of noncompliance, and the organization's particular risk factors.

Monitoring should also include the types of coding that are not typically performed by coding staff, such as the CPT codes listed in the chargemaster. Depending on the findings, subsequent reviews can be narrower in focus. A higher sample of cases in the organization's top DRGs, ambulatory payment classifications (APCs), diagnoses, procedures, and/or clinical services should be reviewed. (See figure 4.) For DRG reviews, cases may be selected in a number of ways.

In addition to evaluating coding accuracy, the completeness of physician documentation to support coding should be monitored.

The organization's internal coding practices should be evaluated to ensure that they are consistent with coding rules and guidelines. If organization-specific coding guidelines

Figure 4.   Examples of various case selections

- Simple random sample
- Medical DRGs by high dollar and high volume
- Surgical DRGs by high dollar and high volume
- Medical DRGs without comorbid conditions or complications
- Surgical DRGs without comorbid conditions or complications
- Major diagnostic category by high dollar and high volume
- Most common diagnosis codes
- Most common procedure codes (ICD-9-CM or CPT)
- Significant procedure APCs by high dollar and high volume
- Unlisted CPT codes
- "Separate procedure" CPT codes reported in conjunction with related CPT codes
- Unusual modifier usage patterns (for example, high volume of CPT codes reported with modifier -59 or modifier -25)
- Not elsewhere classified (NEC) and not otherwise specified (NOS) codes
- Highest-level evaluation and management (E/M) codes
- Chargemaster review by service
- Superbill, encounter form, and charge sheet review by specialty

have been developed, they should be evaluated to ensure that they are not in conflict with official coding guidelines or recently implemented directives. Staff compliance with coding policies and procedures should be continuously reviewed. All systems and software applications that utilize diagnosis and procedure codes should be identified and the code tables reviewed to ensure the codes are accurate and up-to-date.

In addition to coding evaluations, HIM departments need to review the accuracy of other data elements that they share responsibility for and that affect reimbursement or clinical data management (for example, data entry of discharge status, patient's age, admission and discharge dates, clinical performance indicators, and outcomes).

Sample Size and Selection
It is important that a large enough sample size be audited for the results to be statistically valid and reliable. The larger the sample size, the greater the confidence in the results. Sampling should include the following:

- Records representative of current areas of investigative focus

- Records representative of internally-identified problem areas

- Random sampling of records to determine overall accuracy

- A sample of cases in any area that shows a significant variation from benchmarks

Samples should be consistent and measurable. Consistency ensures that audit results can be compared and measurability ensures that the sample is statistically significant and reliable. The steps taken for sample selection should be documented. Also important is documentation of the specific population, any population exclusions, sample selection techniques, and the formula used for determining the sample size. Sample selection methods should be replicable so that results from reviews conducted at different times can be compared. If results indicate an increase in errors, corrective steps should be taken immediately.

Audit Process

Initially, a baseline audit should be conducted, consisting of a fairly large sample, representative of all coding professionals, physicians, and all types of cases treated at the organization. The phrase *all types of cases* means all specialties, medical and surgical cases, and the various healthcare settings under the organization's ownership, including the following:

- Inpatient
- Outpatient surgery
- Emergency department
- Clinic
- Physicians' offices
- Ancillary facilities
- Home health
- Subacute care
- Long-term care
- Rehabilitation

A baseline audit enables providers to judge over time their progress in reducing or eliminating potential areas of vulnerability. Every organization needs to know its own data (that is, characteristic patterns, patient mix, and ICD-9-CM/CPT code and DRG distributions) in order to be able to recognize deviations. For this reason, the OIG recommends that organizations take a snapshot of their operations from a compliance perspective. This snapshot becomes the baseline against which variations are identified and progress in resolving problem areas is monitored. A baseline audit examines the claim development and submission process from registration through claim submission and payment and identifies elements within this process that may contribute to noncompliance or that may need to be the focus of process improvement. This audit will establish a consistent methodology for selecting and examining records. The resulting methodology will then serve as a basis for future monitoring. The OIG suggests that baseline levels for coding practices include the frequency and percentile levels of various diagnosis codes and complications or comorbidities.

Once the baseline audit has been completed, follow-up reviews involving a smaller sample of cases should be conducted periodically, according to the organization's schedule. For high-risk, low-volume services, 100 percent of the records should be evaluated. These subsequent reviews should be conducted at regular intervals (that is, quarterly, semi-annually, and annually) to compare current performance (for example, accuracy of coding or another HIM function) with the baseline and any previous evaluations that have been performed subsequent to the baseline. More frequent monitoring may be performed in areas that have been identified as requiring improvement. The results should be used to monitor the effectiveness of corrective action plans implemented to resolve problems identified during previous audits, which helps to demonstrate the effectiveness of the compliance program as a whole. Audits performed subsequent to the baseline audit should seek to determine if improvements have occurred in problem areas and if the initial baseline level was maintained or significantly deviated from in nonproblem areas.

In order to compare the results of subsequent reviews or audits to the baseline audit, a process needs to be developed for the collection and analysis of results over time. Organizations should conduct trend analysis or longitudinal studies that uncover deviations in specific areas over a given period of time. Comparisons should be made of year-to-year activity or one six-month time period to another. Patterns and potential problem areas often can be identified by reviewing reports (monthly, quarterly, and/or annual) of diagnosis and procedure codes and DRG frequency. Reading such reports should prompt questions like, Are there changes in the outpatient case-mix distribution or coding patterns since the implementation of the outpatient PPS? Whenever possible, reports of auditing and monitoring activities should be maintained electronically to facilitate comparisons of results over time and to identify trends.

Reports providing data on the organization's code or reimbursement category (such as DRG or APC, respectively) frequency and distribution must be designed carefully to ensure that comparisons of apples to apples are being made. (See figure 5.)

Organizations should use comparative data to benchmark utilization and billing patterns with national, state, and regional norms. Comparative data can be used to assist one's organization in evaluating indicator results and determining whether an area should be examined further. Comparative data are available from a number of sources, including CMS, state data commissions, professional associations such as hospital associations, medical societies, and private companies. CMS's MEDPAR data are available as a public use file. (See appendix F for a list of comparative data sources and appendix G for fiscal year 2000 MEDPAR data.) Improbable combinations of codes, unusual trends (including changes in internal patterns), or variations from national, state, or regional norms may indicate areas requiring focused health record review. (See figure 6, page 50.)

Figure 5.   Basic formulas for DRG monitors

- Facility's CC%:

$$\frac{\#\ discharges\ in\ DRGs\ with\ CC}{\#\ discharges\ in\ DRGs\ with\ CC\ +\ \#\ discharges\ in\ DRGs\ without\ CC} \times 100$$

- Facility's DRG Y% of DRGs Y/Z:

$$\frac{\#\ discharges\ in\ DRG\ Y}{\#\ discharges\ in\ DRG\ Y\ +\ \#\ discharges\ in\ DRG\ Z} \times 100$$

- Facility's DRG A/B% of DRGs A/B/C/D:

$$\frac{\#\ discharges\ in\ DRG\ A\ +\ \#\ discharges\ in\ DRG\ B}{(\#\ discharges\ in\ DRG\ A\ +\ \#\ discharges\ in\ DRG\ B)\ +\ (\#\ discharges\ in\ DRG\ C\ +\ \#\ discharges\ in\ DRG\ D)} \times 100$$

When reviewing records, organizations should ensure that the regulatory requirements and payment policies in effect during the applicable time period (as opposed to the regulatory requirements and payment policies in effect at the time the review is performed) are utilized. The consideration should be given to whether the payer required that codes from a different (invalid) version of the code set being reported during the applicable time period. The organization's encoder should not be used to recode records. Problems caused by encoder logic or edits will be missed if the same encoder used to code the records is also used to audit coding accuracy.

Criteria should be established for the types of occurrences that will count as errors (see figure 7). Coding errors can generally be categorized as clerical, judgmental, and systemic. Clerical errors are generally random in nature and occur infrequently. Judgmental errors can be minimized through clear, comprehensive policies and procedures and education. Systemic errors are particularly high-risk for potentially triggering a fraud investigation since they involve patterns of errors. Common coding errors include the following:

- Selecting an incorrect principal diagnosis
- Selecting an incorrect code
- Failing to include or incorrectly including a fifth digit on a diagnosis code
- Coding diagnoses or procedures that are not supported by health record documentation
- Failing to code all diagnoses or procedures that are supported by health record documentation

Figure 6.   Factors to consider when monitoring coding accuracy

---

Reliability: The degree to which the same results are achieved (for example, when different individuals code the same health record, they use the same codes.)

Validity: The degree to which the codes accurately reflect the patient's diagnoses and procedures

Completeness: The degree to which the codes capture all the diagnoses and procedures reflected in the health record

Timeliness: The time frame in which the health records are being coded

---

Figure 7.   Questions to consider when establishing error criteria

---

- Will error rates be calculated and reported as percentages, raw numbers, or proportions?
- Will they include the number of records coded incorrectly or the number of incorrect codes?
- What is meant by an incorrect code (transposition of numbers, missing fourth or fifth digits, wrong code selected)?
- How will the selection of principal diagnosis or other sequencing occurrences be evaluated?
- Will miscoding, incomplete identification of all secondary diagnoses, and incomplete identification of all procedures be calculated differently in the error rate?
- Will errors affecting DRG assignment be treated differently from those that do not?

- Failing to clarify conflicting or ambiguous documentation
- Entering data erroneously into the abstracting or billing system

Common causes of coding errors include the following:

- Missing, inadequate, or conflicting documentation
- Failure to review entire health record
- Insufficient coding education
- Lack of coding knowledge or skills
- Lack of understanding of disease process or procedure
- Misinterpretation of coding rules or guidelines
- Incorrect coding advice
- Lack of or outdated coding resources, codebooks, and/or encoding software
- Failure to stay informed of coding rules and guidelines, reimbursement policies, and regulatory changes
- Lack of familiarity with National Correct Coding Initiative (CCI) edits
- Employment of outdated or inaccurate cheat sheets that incorporate codes
- Use of a record abstract, charge sheet, or superbill instead of the complete health record to assign codes
- Selection of a code for a payable diagnosis instead of assignment of the correct code for the diagnosis documented in the health record
- Use of E/M codes for preventative medicine services in violation of CPT coding guidelines
- Use of an improper modifier
- Adherence to unclear or outdated policies and procedures

Data Collection
The following data elements should be collected as part of the evaluation and monitoring of coding accuracy:

- Admission and discharge dates
- Payer
- Date that the record was originally coded
- Original diagnosis and procedure codes
- Reviewer's diagnosis and procedure codes
- Impact on case designation (that is, did error affect DRG, APC, or home health resource group classification?)

- Impact on reimbursement

- Quality errors

- Root cause of the coding error (for example, lack of adherence to official coding guideline, missed documentation, inconsistent documentation, incomplete documentation, and clerical error)

- Original and reviewer's discharge disposition (for reviews of acute care hospital inpatient records)

- Health record documentation supporting reviewer's codes (note whether documentation was likely to have been present at the time the record was originally coded: for example, a discharge summary dictated after the record was coded)

- Citation or reference to support auditor's coding changes (for example, *Coding Clinic for ICD-9-CM* citation and reference to a specific guideline from the *Official ICD-9-CM Guidelines for Coding and Reporting*)

Retrospective versus Prospective Review

Every healthcare organization will need to decide whether retrospective and/or prospective record reviews of coding accuracy will be conducted. If violations of civil, criminal, or administrative law are identified during a retrospective review, this information must be reported to the federal government. Any problems identified during a retrospective review should be reported promptly to the corporate compliance officer, who, in conjunction with legal counsel, can determine the extent of liability and whether the matter should be reported to government authorities. Any identified overpayments should be refunded to the affected payer with a letter of explanation. A retrospective review offers an opportunity to identify and investigate practice patterns or deviations from national norms before becoming the target of a government investigation. The organization's internal investigation may reveal a reasonable explanation for the variation, which will be useful in the event of a government investigation.

Before conducting a retrospective audit, an organization should carefully consider the benefits and drawbacks and the necessary actions if the audit results identify a possible problem involving overpayments. Once a problem has been discovered, it cannot be ignored. The problem will need to be investigated to determine the extent and the appropriate corrective action—including refunds of overpayments—that must be taken. It is advisable that the organization consult its legal counsel prior to initiating a retrospective audit. If it is determined that a retrospective audit is appropriate, such as in situations when coding problems involving overpayments are suspected, legal counsel can advise as to the retrospective time period that should be covered by the audit in view of the facts and applicable statutes of limitations.

When a prospective review is performed, a sample of records should be reviewed after they have been coded but before the claims have been submitted to the payer. The advantage of a prospective review is that errors can be corrected and corrective action plans initiated for any identified systematic problems before the submission of erroneous claims, thus avoiding the need to refund overpayments.

Internal versus External Review

Coding evaluation and assessment can be conducted either internally or by an outside firm. A combination of these approaches may work best if an organization does not have qualified staff available who work independently from the actual coding function. An external agency is recommended for periodic reviews. Regardless of whether the assessments are conducted internally or externally, a key point is that the review should be conducted by an expert in the area being audited. Individuals performing coding assessments should be familiar with the functions, processes, and rules and guidelines pertaining to coding and health record documentation. They should have several years of coding experience in the applicable coding system(s) and healthcare setting and the appropriate credentials. The reviewer should also be required to demonstrate a practical application of auditing skills and data quality assessment competence.

Regular, ongoing monitoring can be conducted by internal staff and a less frequent formal audit (perhaps annually) by an outside organization. The frequency of an external review depends on the organization's case volume and internal risk assessment. A good external audit of the organization's operations, documentation, and claim submission process can help it evaluate its risk objectively and will produce sound recommendations for implementing a proactive approach to correct any identified problems. An external review often helps promote physician education and awareness and focus on documentation issues and training of coding professionals. Internal monitoring should be performed by an objective entity with adequate training and experience in coding. For example, a coding professional should not review the accuracy of his or her own coding, and a corporate compliance officer who is not an HIM professional or a department director who has not been actively coding for several years is not appropriately qualified to monitor coding accuracy. Organizations can broaden the skills of their coding staff by implementing a peer review monitoring program, whereby coding professionals review each other's work. However, implementation of such a program should not serve as the only method of review. Inter-rater reliability can be measured when the coding professionals recode each other's records. This method is not effective in identifying all types of errors such as those errors or misunderstandings occurring among all the coding professionals. For an organization with few academically trained and/or certified professionals, use of an outside firm for all auditing and monitoring activities may be the only viable option to ensure compliance and maintain acceptable coding accuracy.

Documentation of Process and Results

All auditing and monitoring activities should be documented (see figure 8, page 54). Documentation should include results by individual coding professional and by the coding professionals as a whole group or by clinical specialty, if applicable. Errors should be classified by both type and severity (see figure 9, page 54). Any trends related to availability of documentation at the time of coding should be noted as well as any trends related to the root cause of the coding error. Examples of trends by root cause include an official coding guideline or a coding rule or convention.

Results of auditing and monitoring activities (even if no problem is identified) should be reported to the HIM compliance specialist. In turn, he or she should submit a written report of findings to the corporate compliance officer, who then should share the reports with the following:

- The organization's senior management
- The compliance committee
- The medical staff, if appropriate
- The corporate compliance officer for the parent organization (in those cases where the organization reporting the audit findings is owned by a larger corporate entity)

Figure 8.   Information to document when auditing or monitoring

- Date of review
- Identity of evaluator
- Number of cases reviewed
- Number of errors identified
- Number of errors affecting reimbursement
- Financial impact after balancing overcoding and undercoding
- Identification and categorization of trends by such things as DRG, diagnosis, procedure, physician, coding professional, documentation issue, or discharge disposition
- Review methodology
- Review personnel
- Conclusion
- Action taken
- Follow-up conducted

Figure 9.   Examples of error categorization for a hospital inpatient Medicare coding audit

- Principal diagnosis
- Addition of secondary diagnosis that is not a complication and comorbidity (CC)
- Addition of secondary diagnosis that is a CC
- Deletion of secondary diagnosis that is not a CC
- Delection of secondary diagnosis that is a CC
- Addition of procedure that is not an operating room (OR) procedure
- Addition of procedure that is an OR procedure
- Change in diagnosis code affecting DRG assignment
- Change in diagnosis code not affecting DRG assignment
- Change in procedure code affecting DRG assignment
- Change in procedure code not affecting DRG assignment

Analysis of Results

Once variations have been identified, in-depth reviews can be conducted to determine the reason(s). When problems are identified through the auditing and monitoring process, focused reviews can be conducted that look at a higher volume of cases in these areas on a more frequent basis. Focused reviews aimed at the OIG's identified target areas also should be conducted to determine whether the organization has any problems in these areas. Areas suggesting a need for focused review also can be identified by comparing DRG or code distribution data over time or with local, state, or national figures. Additionally, focused reviews can be designed based on problem areas identified via other mechanisms, such as claims denial patterns or under-reimbursed services. Whenever deviations are discovered, the reasons should always be investigated.

Once an in-depth review confirms that a variation truly is a problem, steps will need to be taken to initiate corrective action and prevent recurrence (see page 61 for the upcoming section titled Problem Resolution and Corrective Action).

Results of ongoing monitoring activities can be used to help focus the audit and investigation processes, including sample selection.

Feedback regarding the results of auditing and monitoring activities should be presented to appropriate individuals such as coding staff and physicians. Statistics by individual coding professionals or type of setting should be maintained, and, when necessary, the coding professional and supervisor should work together to develop an action plan to improve the coding accuracy. In addition, progress in improvements in coding accuracy should be tracked.

The results of the coding reviews should be used to identify any problem areas that may require more frequent or intensive review (for example, a higher volume of records to be reviewed such as 100 percent of a specific diagnosis code). The results of auditing and monitoring activities should be used to identify gaps in knowledge or weak areas, and appropriate training should be provided to address these deficiencies. Depending on the nature of the problem areas, the training might be aimed at the coding staff or the physicians.

Areas of vulnerability in relation to compliance identified through the monitoring process should be examined regularly until it is clear the problem has been corrected. When monitoring discloses that deviations were undetected in a timely manner due to deficiencies in the compliance program, appropriate modifications to the program must be implemented. A comparison of audit results with previous audits should be conducted to identify whether any identified problems have increased, decreased, or remained the same.

When a review of DRG assignment accuracy is conducted (either internally or by an outside company), lower-weighted as well as higher-weighted DRG adjustments should be submitted to the fiscal intermediary. The submission of only higher-weighted DRG adjustments may be viewed as a willful intent to defraud the payer rather than correction of claims for appropriate reimbursement.

Auditing and monitoring processes should encompass claims submitted to private payers and government programs alike. Whenever a review identifies errors that resulted in receipt of incorrect reimbursement (either an overpayment or underpayment), the claim should be resubmitted with the corrected code assignments to the affected payer according to that payer's policy for claim resubmission. If any errors are discovered that resulted in an overpayment, the difference must be refunded to the affected payer. In addition, appropriate documentation and an explanation for the reason for the refund should be included. Refunds for identified overpayments must be returned to the payer even when the time frame for claim resubmission has expired. Also, any errors should be corrected in internal databases and indexes so that correct and consistent code sets are maintained for each encounter or episode. (See figure 10, page 56, for suggestions regarding auditing and monitoring methodologies.)

Figure 10.   Guidelines for the auditing and monitoring of HIM functions

The following guidelines are only suggestions and are not intended to serve as an all-inclusive list.

- Compare diagnosis and procedure codes with health record documentation. If coding is performed without a complete health record, review the coding accuracy after the record is complete to determine if an incomplete record is adversely affecting coding accuracy.

- Compare diagnosis codes with procedure codes for consistency.

- For CPT E/M code assignment, compare the required components of the reported code with the documentation in the health record to ensure that the code level assigned is substantiated.

- For organizations operating under the outpatient PPS, compare the E/M code assignments with the criteria developed by the organization and the health record documentation for the following reasons:

    —To assess the accuracy of the code assignment

    —To ensure that the organization's system for mapping facility services to the E/M code levels is being followed

    —To determine whether supporting documentation is present in the health record.

- Compare the diagnostic information provided by the ordering physician or practitioner for diagnostic tests with the diagnosis codes reported on the claim and, if possible, with the reason for the ordered test documented in the physician's office health record.

- Review medical necessity denials for the following reasons:

    —To determine the accuracy of diagnostic information reported on the claim (Do the diagnosis codes match the diagnostic information provided by the ordering physician or practitioner and documented in his or her office record?)

    —To verify the accuracy of the billed tests (Were the tests that were billed the same as the tests that were ordered and performed?)

    —To ascertain whether an ABN was issued, and, if not, to identify the reason(s) why

- When multiple CPT codes have been assigned, verify that they are not components of a larger, comprehensive procedure that could be described with a single code.

- For Medicare patients, compare the reported CPT codes with the edits in the National CCI.

- Work with physicians to develop a mechanism for comparing the diagnosis and procedure codes assigned by the physician's office and the facility for the same encounter.

- Perform periodic chart-to-bill audits by reviewing representative samples or records coded by different coders or involving different physicians. This may indicate problem areas requiring more intensive review and, possibly, corrective action.

- Evaluate claim denials, claim rejections, and code and DRG changes from the FI, QIO, and private payers.

    —Ensure the APCs assigned by the Medicare contractor and the provider organization are in agreement and investigate any discrepancies.

    —Appeal all denials believed to be inappropriate, even if only small amounts of money are involved.

    —Verify that denials based on the CCI edits are based on current edits and not on a deleted one.

    —Cite any official sources that support the accuracy of the organization's code assignment.

    —Follow up on the issue until a response has been received by the payer.

    —Educate the coding staff if review of the denials, rejections, and code changes indicates a pattern of inaccurate coding.

Figure 10. *(Continued)*

—Monitor claims rejections for patterns of errors and initiate corrective action when a pattern is identified.

–Are modifiers not being used, or being used improperly?

–Are codes being unbundled inappropriately?

–Are duplicate codes being assigned by both the HIM department and ancillary departments?

—Correct any errors in coding and billing practices to prevent future claim denials. High denial rates or repeated coding and billing errors may increase the organization's risk of being audited.

- Perform trend analysis of practice patterns by examining the organization's internal coding and DRG patterns over time and doing the following:

—Look for significant changes in the organization's case mix or coding practices. Sudden increases in an organization's case-mix index or a case-mix index that is high relative to other hospitals with a similar mix of patients and services may serve as a red flag to fraud investigators. Some fluctuation in the case-mix index is to be expected, but a sharp and sustained increase may be considered suspect.

—Identify any DRGs that show substantial increases in the number of cases assigned to them. Compare the DRG distribution, ranked by volume, over the past three years and identify any DRGs that have changed ranking significantly for further, in-depth study. This intensive review should include identifying the reason for the change in ranking.

—Select individual DRGs and compare the previous year to the current year.

—Look at families of related DRGs such as "with CC" and "without CC" pairs or high-risk DRG pairs, examining the case distribution within a family over time.

- Compare utilization and billing patterns with national, state, and regional norms by doing the following:

—Look at the organization's highest- and lowest-volume DRGs and APCs. Compare these DRGs and APCs in terms of volume with norms for the region, state, and nation.

–Look at changes in the volume of patients assigned to particular DRGs and APCs.

—Compare the organization's case distribution within a family with regional, state, and national averages.

- Analyze trends—both over time and against regional, state, and national averages—for CPT procedure codes and APCs. For physician practices, compare the frequency of various levels of E/M codes with other physician practices, particularly those in the same specialty.

- Analyze trends for evidence of inappropriate upcoding.

- Examine any identified variations from norms or over time to determine causes. Variations do not necessarily indicate improper coding practices, so all possible causes should be considered. HIM professionals should take the lead in identifying variations, determining the validity of the coding practices represented by the data, producing explanations for the variations (or at least verifying that they are not due to improper coding), and documenting circumstances resulting in unexpected variations.

- Determine whether the correct discharge status is being reported, particularly for patients transferred to another acute care hospital or to a postacute setting. For patients who will be receiving home health care upon discharge from the acute care facility, confirm that a written plan of care for the provision of home health services documented in the health record. Look for a pattern of discharge status corrections made by the Medicare contractor.

Monitoring the Physician Query Process

The use of queries should be monitored for trends, and education should be provided to physicians on proper documentation of a diagnosis when a pattern of poor documentation is identified. Education is key to improvement and will result in better documentation up front and a reduction in the need to query the physician and then, if necessary, amend the record. Educational programs should include information on the effect documentation has on reimbursement as well as continued patient care. Educational sessions may provide insight into improvements that could be made in documentation capture processes to facilitate better health record practices.

Periodic reviews of the use of queries should include an evaluation of what percentage of the query forms are eliciting negative and positive responses from the physicians. A high negative response rate may indicate that the coding staff are being overzealous and not using the query process judiciously. A high positive response rate may indicate that there are widespread poor documentation habits that need to be addressed. It may also indicate that the absence of certain reports, such as the discharge summary or operative report, at the time of coding is forcing the coding staff to query the physician to obtain the information they need for complete code selection. In this case, it might make more sense, in terms of turn-around time and productivity, to wait for completion of these reports, particularly if they are the primary source for the final diagnoses or the only source of operative session details.

Patterns of poor documentation that have not been addressed through education or other corrective action are signs of an ineffective compliance program. Ideally, complete and accurate physician documentation should occur at the time care is rendered. The need for a query form following patient discharge results from incomplete, conflicting, or ambiguous documentation, which is an indication of poor information capture of patient conditions and events. Therefore, query form usage should be the exception, not the norm. The OIG noted in its *Compliance Program Guidance for Hospitals* that "accurate coding depends upon the quality of completeness of the physician's documentation" and "active staff physician participation in educational programs focusing on coding and documentation should be emphasized by the hospital" (OIG 1998, p. 8995, footnote 43).

The query format should be monitored to ensure that the queries are not leading the physicians to agree to the reporting of additional diagnoses or procedures that are not supported by the health record documentation for the express purpose of higher reimbursement. Patterns of inappropriately written queries may need to be referred to the facility's compliance officer if it appears that overpayment may have resulted as a direct result of this process.

Recurring violations of a facility's own policies and procedures related to the use of physician queries should also be addressed.

Appropriate use of the form, analysis of trends, and follow-up education for identified patterns of documentation deficiencies should lead to a decrease in the need to use a query form. The query process can be used to move the institution and its clinical staff closer to an ideal world in terms of patient care and documentation quality through improvement of future documentation practices, medical error and patient safety monitoring, and quality review.

Auditing of Compliance Program Effectiveness

In order for a compliance program to be effective, it must be evaluated continually in a proactive manner through auditing and monitoring and primarily focus on preventing regulatory requirement violations as well as responding to problems. An effective compliance program should incorporate periodic (at least annual) reviews of adherence to any of its elements (such as participation at educational programs, timely communication of policies and regulatory updates, and disciplinary action when appropriate). The adage "actions speak louder than words" applies in such situations. An organization must demonstrate that it does what its written program states that it does. If the organization does not plan to implement a procedure until a future date, its compliance program should not indicate that this procedure is currently being carried out. To be considered an effective compliance program, there must be evidence of compliance through detecting, correcting, and preventing health information creation and maintenance problems. The federal government has stated that the hallmark of an effective program is that the organization exercised due diligence in seeking to prevent and detect criminal conduct of its employees and other agents. The attributes of each individual element of a compliance program must be evaluated in order to assess the program's effectiveness as a whole.

Evaluating how a compliance program performs during the organization's day-to-day operations is a critical indicator of effectiveness. Do patterns of errors or other identified problems indicate that employees do not understand policies and procedures or coding rules and guidelines? Organizations should consider periodically testing the staff about regulatory rules and guidelines to determine its level of knowledge and comprehension of regulatory requirements, pertinent compliance issues, and the relationship of regulations to the staff's own job tasks. An effective method of evaluating comprehension is to present hypothetical scenarios of situations experienced in daily practice and assess the responses. Evaluation of the effectiveness of the training programs should also be conducted. The organization should answer the following questions:

- How frequently are staff and physicians trained? Are employees tested after training?

- Have documentation practices improved as a result of physician education?

- Do the training sessions and materials adequately summarize the important aspects of the organization's compliance program?

- Are training instructors qualified to present the subject matter and field questions with appropriate answers?

Effective auditing and monitoring is evidenced by how an organization determines the parameters of its reviews. Questions an organization should consider in regard to these parameters include the following:

- Does the audit program encompass all payers and all aspects of proper billing? For example, does a coding audit address both the assignment of correct codes and the presence of complete and accurate documentation, or only the code assignments?

- Are results of past audits, pre-established baselines, or prior deficiencies re-evaluated?

- Are identified problems corrected?

- Are steps taken to correct patterns of poor documentation?

- Are auditing techniques valid and are audits conducted by objective, qualified reviewers?

Results of reviews should be used to revise the compliance program itself in order to improve its effectiveness.

Maintaining documentation of all compliance activities is absolutely key to demonstrating effectiveness of any compliance program. The federal government considers an ineffective program, or one that exists only on paper, as being worse than no compliance program at all.

Enforcement

Because noncompliance is a significant organizational risk, enforcement of adherence to the organization's compliance program is mandatory. Appropriate and consistent disciplinary mechanisms should be instituted for employees or physicians who violate the organization's standards of conduct, policies and procedures, or federal or state laws, or have otherwise engaged in wrongdoing. Any noncompliant behavior, including an employee's failure to detect a violation that is attributable to his or her negligence or reckless conduct, should result in disciplinary action. After a violation is detected, the organization must take all reasonable steps to respond appropriately to the offense and take action to prevent similar offenses in the future, including any necessary modifications to the compliance program. In addition to being appropriate to the circumstances, responses to detected violations should be consistent. In other words, all levels of employees should be subject to the same disciplinary action for the commission of similar offenses. Disciplinary action should be fair and equitable. The organization's managerial staff, compliance officer, and human resource department should work together to develop disciplinary policies that are in accordance with the OIG's expectations (as described in the OIG compliance program guidances). The human resource department's policies pertaining to disciplinary action, including requirements for documentation of disciplinary actions taken, should be consistent with the compliance program, and these policies should be communicated and followed.

The various levels of disciplinary action (up to and including termination) that may be imposed on executives, managers, employees, physicians, and independent contractors for failure to comply with standards, policies, statutes, and regulations should be clearly spelled out and communicated to all involved. The individual responsible for carrying out each level of disciplinary action also should be determined (such as a supervisor, a human resource representative, or a member of administration).

For new employees being hired to fill positions that carry discretionary authority to make decisions involving compliance with the law (including coding professionals and the HIM compliance specialist), a reasonable and prudent background investigation should be conducted. The investigation should include a careful check of references.

Managers, supervisors, medical staff, and others in a supervisory capacity should be held accountable for failing to comply with, or encouraging or directing employees to violate, regulatory requirements. The applicable standards, procedures, and laws should be followed by everyone. The appropriate manager or supervisor should be disciplined for failing to adequately instruct his or her subordinates or to detect noncompliance with applicable policies and regulations. When it has been determined that reasonable diligence on his or her part would have led to the discovery of a problem, a manager is obligated to provide the organization an opportunity to correct it. Adherence to the provisions of the compliance program should also be a factor in every employee's annual performance evaluation. Contractual agreements, with either individuals or companies, should stipulate that the contracted entity's failure to comply with the organization's standards of conduct, policies and procedures, and federal and state laws and regulations is cause for immediate termination of the contract.

Problem Resolution and Corrective Action

The healthcare organization must be able to demonstrate that reasonable steps have been taken to achieve compliance with policies, standards, and regulatory requirements and that all reports of perceived violations disclosed by employees or others are investigated and appropriate actions taken. Reasonable steps must be taken to resolve any identified problems and ensure that similar problems do not recur. When a potential problem or unusual trend is identified, through either the review process or some other mechanism (such as employee identification or external agency notification), an internal investigation should be undertaken to determine its cause, scope, and consequences. The HIM compliance specialist should be involved in all internal investigations of coding issues or other HIM concerns and determination of subsequent corrective action.

Organizations should consider developing a set of warning indicators that trigger further review to determine if a problem exists. Triggers might include the following:

- Significant changes in the number and/or types of claim rejections and/or reductions

- Correspondence from payers challenging the medical necessity or validity of claims

- Illogical patterns or unusual changes in the pattern of HCPCS or ICD-9-CM code utilization

When a trend is evident, it should be determined whether the trend is related to clinical factors, data management, or coding practices and if the issue is isolated, limited to a given time period, or an ongoing problem. If the trend appears to be coding related, all pertinent policies and procedures, regulations, and official coding guidelines should be reviewed to determine whether the coding practice is improper. The review may reveal that a trend can be explained by a change in a code or coding guideline. If the review is inconclusive as to whether the coding practice in question is improper, an official source should be contacted for further information: a Cooperating Party organization if it is an ICD-9-CM–related issue or the AMA if it is a CPT-related issue. The coding errors may be related to poor documentation or the coding process (for example, coding without all necessary documentation available). The organization should consider whether encoder software logic or information system planning is a factor in the identified errors. Staff should be interviewed to determine how the practice might have started. For example, a new coding professional or supervisor, consultant, or instructor may have initiated the practice or implemented a new software program for claims processing.

A statistically valid sample of cases should be reviewed to determine whether the problem is isolated (that is, having occurred during a set time period) or widespread and ongoing. All the facts are needed to develop a reasonable explanation regarding the practice's development and to determine the best course of action to correct the situation. This can be accomplished by interviewing staff and/or researching the issue. Possible factors such as initiation of a new service provided by the organization, addition of a specialist to the medical staff, loss of a specialist on the medical staff, a new or revised code, a DRG revision, or a new or revised coding guideline should be considered. The coding staff may have attended a seminar around the time the change in coding practice occurred or a consultant may have conducted a coding review. Perhaps a change in patient mix has occurred or a procedure that was usually performed on an inpatient basis has shifted to the outpatient setting, or vice versa.

Changes in reimbursement methodology may also be a relevant factor. For example, implementation of the outpatient prospective payment system, as well as other prospective payment systems, is likely to result in changes in utilization and coding and billing patterns. Procedures previously performed as an outpatient may shift now to the inpatient setting because they are part of the CMS's "inpatient only" list. CPT codes previously reported separately may be bundled now as part of the CCI edits. Significant volume decreases in high-volume, low-weight DRGs can result in an increase in the organization's overall case-mix index. Changes in the case-mix index may have occurred because a physician with several patients in a high-volume, low-weight DRG left the medical staff, or perhaps utilization review has successfully encouraged physicians to utilize observation services for some of the patients assigned to a specific DRG. If the frequency of assignment of the critical care codes has increased significantly, perhaps the physicians received education on the proper use of these codes and now do a better job of documenting time spent rendering critical care. Perhaps the number of critical care beds has increased or the physician's practice has shifted such that he has more critical care patients. Or perhaps an individual coding professional misunderstands the proper use of the critical care codes and he or she is assigning a critical care code whenever a patient occupies an intensive care unit (ICU) or critical care unit (CCU) bed.

If a reasonable explanation for the pattern or aberration is found, the reason should be documented along with the evidence and official resources to support it so that it can be readily produced in the event of a fraud investigation. When a legitimate explanation for the deviation is found, and no improper activity is indicated, no corrective action may be necessary.

Once an internal investigation has concluded that a problem exists, corrective action should be promptly initiated to ensure that the identified problem does not recur. Internal organizational policy should dictate the point at which the corporate compliance officer is to become involved. Internal policy also should stipulate the appropriate course of action regarding various types of violations. The specific action that should be taken depends on the circumstances of the situation. In some cases, this might consist of simply generating a repayment to the affected payer with an appropriate explanation. In certain situations, consultation with a coding or billing expert may be helpful in order to determine the best course of action. Corrective action might include new or revised policies and procedures, additional education, disciplinary action, additional edits in encoders or other computer systems (such as a feature of a claims processing system that causes codes to be re-sequenced or dropped entirely), process improvements, or disciplinary action. Education may consist of targeted education for a coding professional or physician, or education on a particular diagnosis, procedure, or coding rule or guideline. All of a coding professional's work or a physician's documentation may need to be reviewed until the problem has been resolved. The particular problem area may need to be monitored on an ongoing basis, such as reviewing 100 percent of the records with a certain diagnosis code. An internal coding policy may need to be revised or developed to prevent recurrence of the problem. The type and urgency of corrective action depends on the severity of the problem, including the impact on reimbursement and the prevalence of the problem. While any corrective action taken as the result of an internal investigation will necessarily vary depending on the organization and the specific situation, every organization should strive for some consistency by utilizing sound practices and disciplinary protocols.

Once a problem related to coding errors has been identified, the organization must determine whether overpayments resulted from claims submitted with the errors. Whenever an overpayment is identified, regardless of whether it is due to an honest error or potential fraud, it should be reported to a manager or the corporate compliance officer, according to the organization's reporting policy. Organizations should develop refund and disclosure policies to ensure that any detected violations are handled consistently.

Types of errors and violations should be categorized according to severity, and the appropriate actions to take regarding each category should be clearly delineated in the organization's policies and procedures. For example, a clear, consistent policy should be in place outlining the circumstances for which a simple refund of an overpayment will be made to the payer versus reporting the incident to the federal government.

Follow-up audits should be conducted to ensure that the corrective action has been successful and the problem resolved. The organization should develop a checklist for all identified errors and deficiencies that need to be addressed. Each deficiency should have a follow-up plan associated with it and be backed up by documentation that the plan has been completed and there is evidence that an acceptable level of improvement has been made. Improvement can be evidenced through testing, ongoing monitoring between audits, and follow-up auditing. If a follow-up audit shows little or no improvement, modifications to the corrective action plan may be required.

If the results of an investigation reveal evidence of misconduct that may violate criminal, civil, or administrative law, then the issue should be promptly reported to a government authority within a reasonable period of time (not more than sixty days after determining there is credible evidence of a violation). The OIG has indicated that instances of noncompliance must be determined on a case-by-case basis and that the existence or amount of a monetary loss to a healthcare program is not solely determinant of whether the conduct should be investigated and reported to governmental authorities. In fact, in some instances when there is no monetary loss to a healthcare program, corrective action and reporting to governmental authorities is still necessary to protect the integrity of the applicable healthcare program and its beneficiaries. The OIG believes that some violations may be so serious that they warrant immediate notification to governmental authorities, prior to, or simultaneous with, commencing an internal investigation, such as the following instances:

- Clear violations of criminal law
- Conduct that has a significant adverse effect on the quality of care

- Evidence of a systemic failure to comply with applicable laws, an existing corporate integrity agreement, or other standards of conduct, regardless of the financial impact on the healthcare program

Regardless of the organization's specific policy on self-reporting to the government, any identified overpayments (from any payer) should be refunded promptly to the applicable payer. Failure to repay overpayments within a reasonable period of time could be interpreted as an intentional attempt to conceal the overpayment, thereby establishing an independent basis for a criminal violation with respect to the organization, as well as any individuals who may have been involved.

After an internal investigation has confirmed the existence of a problem, the HIM compliance specialist, in conjunction with HIM staff, should review the circumstances related to the issue and make every effort to identify and investigate similar or related areas. For example, if an internal investigation uncovers the overcoding of complications or comorbidities in one pair of DRGs, it would be logical to look at other CC/non-CC DRG pairs to see whether overcoding occurred elsewhere.

All aspects of the internal investigation should be documented. Records of the investigation should contain the following elements:

- Documentation of the alleged violation

- A description of the investigative process

- Copies of notes from interviews with staff, physicians, and/or external entities

- Copies of key documents such as a pertinent coding guideline or a *Coding Clinic for ICD-9-CM* reference

- A log of the people interviewed and the documents reviewed

- The results of the investigation (for example, any disciplinary action taken and/or corrective action implemented)

Records of the investigation should be maintained by the corporate compliance officer. The HIM compliance specialist, under the direction of the corporate compliance officer, should take appropriate steps at the initiation of an internal investigation to prevent the destruction or loss of documents or other evidence relevant to the investigation.

Unique Considerations for Healthcare Settings Other Than the Acute Care Inpatient Setting

Some of the unique issues pertaining to development of HIM compliance programs in certain types of nonacute care healthcare settings are described in the following sections.

Hospital Outpatient Services

The implementation of the outpatient prospective payment system (OPPS) has made accurate documentation and coding critically important in the hospital outpatient setting. In addition to the impact on appropriate reimbursement, accuracy is also important because the billing data reported by hospitals will be used to revise weights and other adjustments that will affect APC payments in future years. While HCPCS codes and modifiers directly impact reimbursement, diagnosis codes are important for justifying the medical necessity of the services rendered. Additionally, once CMS implements an observation APC for reimbursement of observation services for certain diagnoses, the accuracy of the code assignments for the diagnoses classified to the observation APC will be important in order to ensure reimbursement under this APC. Since certain diagnostic tests are required for the conditions classified to the observation APC, accurate documentation and reporting of these tests is extremely important.

Since CMS is allowing hospitals to develop their own systems for reporting CPT E/M codes for emergency and clinic visits, each hospital must be able to demonstrate that it is following its own system and that the facility's system reasonably relates the intensity of resources to the different levels of E/M codes. Determining the appropriate E/M level depends on thorough documentation by physicians, nurses, and other clinical personnel of all observations, diagnoses, treatments, and medical decision-making. There are a number of actions hospitals can take to ensure compliance with OPPS requirements (Stewart 2001, pp. 58–60):

- Physicians should undergo training regarding their obligations for accurate and complete documentation in the health record. The goal is to improve documentation in order to capture all diagnoses and procedures performed and ensure accurate and complete coding.

- HIM staff should receive training on health record review methods for appropriate assignment of ICD-9-CM and HCPCS codes and modifiers.

- The chargemaster should be reviewed and updated annually to ensure accurate reporting of those ancillary and other items and/or services generated by the chargemaster. This review should involve all of the departments whose services are represented on the chargemaster.

- Registration personnel should receive training on LMRP requirements and procedures for obtaining ABNs. Policies should be in place to obtain symptoms or diagnoses from the ordering physician for all ancillary testing or other procedures performed before the patient undergoes the test or procedure.

- E/M code assignments should be compared with the criteria developed by the hospital and the health record documentation to assess the accuracy of the code assignments, to ensure that the hospital's system for mapping facility services to the E/M code levels is being followed, and to determine whether the code assignments are supported by documentation in the health record.

- HIM staff should ensure that diagnosis codes are consistent with procedure codes and that health record documentation supports reported diagnosis and procedure codes. When multiple CPT codes have been assigned, staff should verify that the codes are not components of a larger, comprehensive procedure that could be described with a single code. CPT code assignments should be checked against the edits in the National CCI.

- HIM staff should ensure the APCs assigned by the Medicare contractor and the hospital are in agreement and any discrepancies should be investigated. All denials believed to be inappropriate should be appealed, even if only small amounts of money are involved. Staff should verify that denials based on CCI edits are based on current edits and not on deleted edits. Official sources that support the accuracy of the hospital's code assignment should be cited. Staff should follow up on the issue until a response has been received by the payer. If review of the denials, rejections, and code changes indicates a pattern of inaccurate coding, this information should be used to provide education to the coding staff. Claims rejections should be monitored for patterns of errors and corrective action should be initiated when a pattern is identified. The proper usage of modifiers should be evaluated, as well as whether codes are being improperly unbundled. It should be determined whether duplicate codes are being assigned by both the HIM department and ancillary departments. Any errors in coding and billing practices must be corrected to prevent future claims denials. High denial rates or repeated coding and billing errors may increase the hospital's risk of being audited by external agencies.

Physician Practices

The OIG noted that one of the most important physician practice compliance issues is the appropriate documentation of diagnoses and treatment. "Timely, accurate, and complete documentation is critical to nearly every aspect of a physician practice" (OIG 2000, p. 36822). In the draft of the OIG's *Compliance Program Guidance for Individual Physicians and Small Group Practices,* the OIG has noted that accurate health record documentation should comply, at a minimum, with the following principles (OIG 2000, pp. 36822–3):

- The medical record should be complete and legible.

- The documentation of each patient encounter should include the reason for the encounter; any relevant history; physical examination findings; prior diagnostic test results; assessment, clinical impression, or diagnosis; plan of care; and date and legible identity of the observer.

- If not documented, the rationale for ordering diagnostic and other ancillary services should [either be documented or] easily inferred by an independent reviewer or third party. Past and present diagnoses should be accessible to the treating and/or consulting physician.

- Appropriate health risk factors should be identified. The patient's progress, his or her response to, and any changes in, treatment, and any revision in diagnosis should be documented.

The OIG has emphasized that (1) the CPT and ICD-9-CM codes reported on the health insurance claim form should be supported by documentation in the physician's office health record, (2) the health record should contain all required information, and (3) CMS and the local carriers should be able to determine who provided the services (OIG 2000, p. 36823). Policies and procedures should be developed to ensure proper completion of the health insurance claim form. The single most appropriate diagnosis code should be linked with the corresponding procedure code and modifiers should be used appropriately. Forms used to capture clinical information should be periodically updated to ensure they elicit the data required for accurate coding. A policy or procedure should be established on the creation and ongoing maintenance of encounter forms (or superbills).

Encounter forms must be kept up-to-date with all ICD-9-CM, CPT, and HCPCS code changes. They must be well designed so that they serve as a tool to improve documentation and do not inappropriately lead to the choice of a particular code. These forms should reflect the common diagnoses and services provided and ordered by the physician practice. Off-the-shelf models should not be used as is, but can serve as a model to design a customized form that is suited to the practice's unique mix of providers, services, payers, and patients. Make sure that codes and code descriptions are complete, valid, and accurate, and that space is allowed to write in additional tests, procedures, and diagnoses if none of the provided choices is appropriate. The design of encounter forms should not encourage selection of the closest code when a code exists that describes the diagnosis or procedure more accurately. Encounter forms should be reviewed at least annually to ensure they are accurate and up-to-date. (See figure 11, page 68.)

The OIG suggests that if a physician practice works with a physician practice management company, independent practice association, physician-hospital organization, management services company, or third-party billing company, the physician practice can incorporate the compliance standards and procedures of those entities, if appropriate, into its own standards and procedures. This material should be tailored to the physician practice.

Figure 11.   Problems that cause focused payer reviews

The more a medical practice understands and abides by documentation requirements and CPT principles, the more it minimizes the risk of adverse consequences from external review. But because of concerns about "upcoding" of physician service levels, it helps to be cautious. Here's a list of problems that may cause a focused payer review:

- **Using the same code over and over.** A physician can easily trigger an audit by using the same level of code repeatedly—for example, using 99213 for office visits, 99223 for hospital admits, and 99244 for office consults. A pattern such as this is easy to detect and shows the physician is not discriminating [levels of care] within the coding system

- **Inconsistencies within partners in a group.** A statistical comparison of partners in a practice shows inconsistent physician education about coding guidelines.

- **Upcoding/undercoding.** In some instances, physicians consistently tend to select higher-level codes. This presents data that is hard to believe and may trigger an audit or review. Two codes the federal government will focus on are 99214 (established patient office visit, level 4) and 99233 (subsequent hospital care, level 3, highest level). It is critical that organizations review their current use of these codes for appropriateness. Undercoding may not trigger an audit but results in lost revenue and creates data quality concerns. For example, some physicians use lower-level codes because they do not want to "bother" with the documentation requirements of the higher levels. This presents a false picture of patient severity and the associated physician work and may actually decrease reimbursement amounts in the future.

- **Modifiers.** Using modifiers correctly can help support documentation and claims in unusual or specific circumstances. When they are used incorrectly—for example, to force a claim to pass edits in place to reject services—modifiers can create a compliance liability. In the physician setting, modifier -25 is especially problematic because it may allow payment for a visit and a procedure when the two services are really not distinct from each other.

- **Diagnoses issues.** Using nonspecific diagnoses or terminology increases the risk of audit for providing unnecessary services. Encourage physicians to use specific diagnoses and document all complications and comorbidities when completing a patient record and ordering specific tests or treatments.

Source: Reprinted from Skurka 2001, p. 52.

Auditing and Monitoring in Physician Practices

Physician practices should first conduct a baseline audit that examines the claim development and submission process and identifies elements within the process that may contribute to noncompliance or that may need to be the focus for improving education. The OIG recommends that the audit be conducted based on claims submitted during the initial three months after implementation of the education and training program so as to give the physician practice a benchmark against which to measure future compliance effectiveness. Periodic reviews should be performed to determine whether claims are accurately coded and accurately reflect the services provided, services or items provided are reasonable and necessary, and health records contain sufficient documentation to support the codes and charges reported on the claim. These periodic audits should be conducted at least once a year and should include (OIG 2000, p. 36827):

- A valid sample of the practice's top ten denials or top ten services
- A review of nonspecific codes to determine if a more specific code would be appropriate
- A check for data entry errors
- Confirmation that all orders are written and signed by a physician
- Confirmation that all tests ordered by the physician were actually performed and documented and that only these tests were billed
- A review of the modifiers assigned

One methodology for identifying the claims or services from which to draw a random sample of claims to be audited is to select the sample from either all of the claims or services a physician has received reimbursement for or all claims or services for a particular payer. Another method is to select the sample from risk areas or potential billing vulnerabilities. Review of the claims requires attention to the distribution of codes used by each physician, and among specialty groups, within the practice to identify variations. These are only a few suggestions based on the practice's assessment of its own risks and the risk areas identified by government agencies and payers. There are many other possible areas that might be appropriate to evaluate.

A physician practice that consistently reports higher-level E/M codes than other practices in the area stands a good chance of catching the attention of fraud investigators. Organizations may consider comparing the frequency of utilization of specific E/M codes between different time periods (for example, two years or two, six-month time periods). They may also compare the utilization of critical care codes between two time periods to identify variations. Periodic, random chart reviews and analysis of coded data provide needed feedback about individual physician coding practices. Physicians should consider all systematic errors or trends in coding or documentation revealed by the chart review. When performing an internal review, it is helpful to have consistent parameters. If a re-evaluation is being performed six months or one year later, results of the first review should be evaluated and cases selected accordingly. If a physician scores particularly well in the first review, fewer cases (perhaps five to seven) can be reviewed the next time around.

If a physician scores poorly in the first review and corrective action has been taken, the same number of records should be reviewed as for the first evaluation. Records documented after the corrective action or educational process has taken place should be selected. All of these processes are part of the cycle of improving the quality of coded data. This data, in turn, will be integrated with financial data to produce information needed to make important decisions about patient care and profitability of providing selected health services. For these reasons, accuracy and completeness are essential, and they begin with documentation in the health record. For physician practices, the OIG recommends that a basic guide for the sample size of periodic random audits is two to five health records per payer or five to ten health records per physician.

During an E/M review process, it is never useful to merely indicate that some codes were "too high" or "too low." Instead, the review should show how increased history, increased physical documentation, or additional documentation of decision-making make it necessary to move patients to higher code levels. This gives physicians more specific guidance on areas that may not be well documented in the record.

New versus Established Patients

Use of the E/M codes for new versus established patients can be a source of coding errors in physician practices. CPT defines a *new patient* as one who has not received any professional services from the physician or another physician of the same specialty who belongs to the same group practice, within the past three years. An *established patient* is one who has received professional services from the physician or another physician of the same specialty who belongs to the same group practice, within the past three years. In the instance where a physician is on call for, or covering for, another physician, the patient's encounter is classified as it would have been by the physician who is not available.

Consultations

Consultations are another potential source of confusion for physician practices, and, therefore, the use of the consultation E/M codes should be monitored for appropriateness. According to CPT, a *consultation* is defined as a type of service provided by a physician whose opinion or advice regarding evaluation or management of a specific problem is requested by another physician or other appropriate source. A confirmatory consultation is one when the consulting physician is aware of the confirmatory nature of the opinion sought (for example, when a second or third opinion is requested or required on the necessity or appropriateness of a previously recommended medical treatment or surgical procedure). Confusion over code selection occurs between new patients, patients whose attending physician has requested advice from a consulting physician, and patients specifically referred to a physician for evaluation and treatment. Many focused reviews have been performed because of potentially erroneous consultation coding and documentation.

Critical Care

Reporting of CPT critical care codes is another risk area for physician practices that requires close monitoring to ensure they are being reported accurately. Critical care is direct care delivered by a physician for a critically ill or injured patient, usually, but not always, rendered in a critical care area such as an intensive care unit (ICU), pediatric ICU, respiratory care unit, or emergency care facility. In CPT, these services are completely time-based. The actual time spent with the patient is the basis for selecting the most appropriate code reflecting the services rendered. The high complexity definition of the critical care codes is assumed to cover the assessment of all possible body system failures or vital organ failure. Physicians report one service or the other: a code from the critical care series or the emergency department visit series but not both for the same episode of care.

It is key for physicians not to separately bill for services included within a critical care CPT code. It is assumed that physicians are performing activities such as interpreting cardiac output measurements, reviewing information stored in computers, and assessing ventilator management as well as performing vascular access procedures, for example, as a part of the critical care services. Audit problems emerge when the physicians or facility bill these services incorrectly. To avoid these issues, the actual time spent with the individual patient should be recorded in the patient's record. This represents good documentation practice, providing adequate documentation supporting the selected CPT code. In addition, physician documentation should extend beyond traditional activities conducted at the bedside to time spent with family members and time spent at the nursing unit with other clinical staff.

Sample audit tools can be found on the floppy disk included with this book. Additionally, sample audit forms for E/M coding and emergency services coding are available to AHIMA members through the AHIMA library on the Communities of Practice Web site (www.ahimanet.org).

Home Health

"The implementation of the Home Health Prospective Payment System (PPS) on October 1, 2001, has presented some unique compliance risks for HIM and billing managers" (Abraham 2001, p. 47). In the home health setting, documentation should record the activity leading to the record entry, the identity of the individual providing the service, and any information needed to support medical necessity and other applicable reimbursement coverage criteria. Since select diagnoses impact the clinical dimension in the home health resource groups (HHRGs), resulting in a direct impact on reimbursement, accurate ICD-9-CM coding is critical. Some diagnoses affecting the clinical dimension can never be reported as the principal or primary diagnosis, according to ICD-9-CM coding rules. These diagnoses are represented by manifestation codes and ICD-9-CM rules require the code for the etiology to be sequenced first. In those instances when ICD-9-CM rules stipulate the proper sequencing of an etiology/manifestation pair of codes, accurate coding of both the etiology and manifestation is required in order to ensure proper reimbursement. According to the home health PPS regulation, the manifestation codes affecting HHRG assignment, which cannot be sequenced as the first diagnosis, must be reported as the first secondary diagnosis in order to impact the clinical dimension of the HHRGs. In this circumstance, the primary diagnosis is indicated by the combination of the manifestation code (in the first secondary diagnosis field) and the code for the underlying disease (in the primary diagnosis field).

Even when the reported ICD-9-CM diagnosis codes do not impact the clinical dimension in the home health case-mix system, they support medical necessity of the home health services provided. Complete and accurate coding of the primary and secondary diagnoses also ensures the collection of accurate data for refinement of the case-mix system.

Agencies are required to determine the primary diagnosis based on the condition that is most related to the current plan of care. The primary or principal (depending on which reporting form is being referred to) diagnosis and the first secondary diagnosis must match on OASIS, the plan of care (HCFA-485), and the claim (HCFA-1450). The primary/principal diagnosis may or may not be related to the patient's most recent hospital stay but must relate to the services rendered by the agency. If more than one diagnosis is treated concurrently, the diagnosis that represents the most acute condition and requires the most intensive services should be reported.

Reportable secondary diagnoses are all conditions that coexisted at the time the plan of care was established, that developed subsequently, or that affect the treatment or care. Diagnoses that relate to an earlier episode and have no bearing on the current plan of care should be excluded.

Only diagnoses and conditions that relate to the patient's current plan of care and treatment should be reported. All reported codes must be supported by physician documentation in the health record. Lack of physician documentation for codes that impact HHRG assignment causes a serious compliance risk. Codes for conditions that are resolved, healed, or no longer affect the patient's plan of care should not be reported. If clarification of a diagnosis is necessary, the physician should be contacted. If clarification of a diagnosis is received from the physician over the telephone, it should be documented as a verbal order in the patient's health record.

Compliance risks in the home health setting include upcoding or downcoding (for example, improper selection of the primary diagnosis or reporting an incorrect code for the primary diagnosis) and improper sequencing (for example, reporting a secondary diagnosis as the primary diagnosis or disregarding mandatory ICD-9-CM rules regarding proper sequencing). Conducting regular ICD-9-CM coding audits in which health record documentation is checked against the codes is crucial to ensure compliance with the Medicare PPS. Such audits of coding data should be performed on a regular basis. In this way, errors or patterns of errors can be identified, and processes can be monitored. Educating administrators, key managers, and the governing board is important to achieve full support for auditing. Managers and supervisors need to understand that coding reviews and audits can benefit the organization in the following ways:

- Improve operational efficiency

- Mitigate damages in the event of an investigation

- Protect against certain legal exposures

- Improve data quality overall

- Ensure reliable data for outcome-based quality management reporting

The OIG recommends that a process be established and maintained for presubmission and postsubmission review of claims (a valid statistical sample) to ensure that claims submitted for reimbursement accurately represent medically necessary services actually provided, supported by sufficient documentation, and in conformity with any applicable coverage criteria for reimbursement (for example, plan of care is dated and signed by the physician; beneficiary is homebound; skilled service is required). Oversight mechanisms should be put in place to ensure that homebound status, as required for Medicare home health coverage, is verified and the specific factors qualifying the patient as homebound are properly documented. Prompts or nursing note forms might help to ensure complete documentation of a patient's homebound status.

Due to the reliance of the home health PPS on OASIS data, it is imperative that measures be taken to ensure that the OASIS data are complete and accurate. There are concerns that payments based on episodes of care could create new incentives to either reduce the amount of services provided to patients or to characterize patients as sicker than they really are, resulting in either overpayments or underpayments. Since OASIS links the patient's clinical status to payment, accurate data are needed to ensure that home health agencies are reimbursed appropriately. Since the primary and secondary diagnoses are reported using ICD-9-CM codes, OASIS data must be supported by documentation in the health record.

As part of its 2001 fiscal year work plan (OIG 2001a, pp. 6–8), OIG aims to examine the effects of OASIS implementation on quality of care and reimbursement. This goal will require careful review of (1) the agencies' assessment processes, (2) the influence assessments have over care plan development, and (3) case-mix accuracy. As a part of their assessment process, agencies conduct initial and periodic assessments of patients' functional capacity. The information gathered in these assessments helps establish the case-mix adjustment. It is from the case-mix adjustment that the level of Medicare payment to a home health agency for a particular patient is established.

Since the design of the home health PPS and the OIG's current enforcement focus in the home health arena will mean an increased emphasis on the importance of data quality, "agencies must design assessment forms and assessment protocols with data quality in mind, and they can prevent unwanted scrutiny by implementing procedures to monitor data entry and data quality" (Abraham 2001, p. 47). Auditing and monitoring activities should encompass the quality of the health record documentation and whether the record supports the billed services. For example, were the services the physician ordered appropriately delivered? If not, is there appropriate documentation or a new physician's order to explain why? Are all billed home health visits supported by health record documentation?

Nursing Facilities

In nursing facilities, a records system should be developed and implemented that ensures complete and accurate health record documentation. Policies should provide for the complete, accurate, and timely documentation of all nursing and therapy services, including subcontracted services, as well as MDS information. The records system should address all records and documentation required for participation in federal, state, and private healthcare programs, including the resident assessment instrument, the comprehensive plan of care, and all corrective actions taken in response to surveys. As part of their compliance programs, nursing facilities need to ensure the following:

- Policies and procedures are in place to ensure accurate and timely assessments.

- Resident classifications match the bills submitted to government payers.

- Facility staff receive training on how to complete the resident assessments.

- Review and auditing mechanisms are in place to check the accuracy and timeliness of the assessments and the adequacy of health record documentation.

Health record documentation should be compared with MDS data to ensure consistency and accuracy, and documentation should support the resource utilization group (RUG) assigned. Policies and procedures will need to be developed and implemented that:

- Establish time frames for completion of the MDS

- Evaluate possible impediments to timely MDS completion

- Evaluate whether current software will continue to meet the needs of the facility under the prospective payment system

- Develop a system to review the accuracy of health record documentation against the MDS data

- Provide focused training on MDS completion and health record documentation necessary to support MDS data

Health record documentation should support the medical necessity and the level of service provided and billed. Falsification and backdating of records should be prohibited and organizations should develop clear standards, consistent with applicable professional and legal standards, that delineate those individuals with the authority to make entries in the health record and the circumstances when late entries may be made in a record. Nursing facilities should formulate policies and procedures that include periodic clinical reviews, both prior and subsequent to billing for services, as a means of verifying that patients are receiving only medically necessary services and that assessments are accurate. For issues pertaining to consolidated billing requirements, there should be established communication mechanisms in place to ensure that duplicative billing does not occur.

Auditing and monitoring activities should encompass the quality of the health record documentation and whether it supports the billed services. For example, are billed services supported by appropriate physician's orders and does the documentation support medical necessity and verify that services were provided? For therapy services provided under Medicare Part A, a physician plan of care must be signed prior to billing, making this an area to audit and monitor. For Part B billing, services are reported with CPT and HCPCS codes. Compliance issues include appropriate code selection, health record documentation that supports the reported codes, proper certification and recertification for therapy services, and documented physician's orders that support the services rendered.

Complete and accurate ICD-9-CM coding of diagnoses is important in the nursing facility setting, as these codes support medical necessity of the care provided. The codes also provide accurate data necessary for research and health policy decisions regarding the provision of care in nursing facilities. Certain specialized services provided in nursing facilities (such as therapy services) are often contracted. The organization's compliance program should stipulate specific elements of these contractual relationships, such as assuring that the contracted staff has the necessary qualifications; receives ongoing education and training regarding proper documentation and new or revised regulatory requirements; and is aware of its responsibility pertaining to accurate documentation and billing of its services. Likewise, the organization must ensure that the vendor has adequate quality control mechanisms in place and agrees to abide by the organization's compliance program.

Inpatient Rehabilitation Facilities

The implementation of a PPS for inpatient rehabilitation facilities has led to new compliance opportunities as reimbursement in the rehabilitation setting is now affected by documentation and coding practices. In the past, documentation practices have not been as thoroughly scrutinized in rehabilitation units and facilities as in acute care hospitals because reimbursement was not based on coding. Now, since reimbursement depends on the information recorded on the patient assessment instrument (PAI), which includes the rehabilitation impairment group code that describes the primary reason for admission to the rehabilitation facility, ICD-9-CM codes for the etiologic diagnosis (pathologic process underlying the impairment condition for which the patient is being admitted to the rehabilitation program) and comorbidities, documentation by physicians, nurses, therapists, and other clinical staff must be reviewed to ensure the information is recorded in a timely and accurate manner. As records are reviewed in the future for proper coding, it is important that the documentation for each episode of care match the appropriate service dates and that there is clear delineation within the different phases of rehabilitative care. Appropriate designation of the rehabilitation impairment group is essential for correct reimbursement. All PAI items must be supported by documentation in the patient's health record.

Certain comorbidities have been designated as conditions that will impact reimbursement and they have been further categorized into high-cost, medium-cost, and low-cost tiers. Under the rehabilitation PPS, comborbidities are defined as conditions that are secondary to the patient's principal diagnosis or rehabilitation impairment group. Accurate coding of these comorbidities, and the existence of health record documentation to support the reported codes, is essential for appropriate reimbursement and for satisfaction of an audit. Incomplete or inaccurate documentation may result in inaccurate code assignment or missed coding opportunities. Facilities will need to make sure their coding staff are properly trained in coding rules and guidelines. Discrepancies between instructions for reporting codes on the claim form and the PAI will create additional challenges for coding staff.

Complications, defined under the rehabilitation PPS as medical conditions that were recognized or identified during the rehabilitation stay and which delayed or compromised the effectiveness of the rehabilitation program or represent high-risk medical disorders, are also reported on the PAI using ICD-9-CM codes. Complications currently do not impact reimbursement, but it is important to code and report them accurately because this data will be used by CMS as part of its ongoing research and to determine what, if any, refinements should be made to the PPS payment rates.

The ICD-9-CM codes on the PAI and claim form do not have to match. On the PAI, the etiologic diagnosis is reported, whereas on the claim form (HCFA-1450), the principal diagnosis is reported. These data elements have different definitions, as do *comorbidities* on the PAI and *secondary diagnoses* on the HCFA-1450.

Compliance risks in the rehabilitation setting include reporting an incorrect rehabilitation impairment group, incorrect coding and reporting of comorbidities, and lack of health record documentation to support the etiologic diagnosis or comorbidities. All reported codes must be supported by physician documentation in the health record. All diagnoses should be coded completely and accurately, regardless of their current impact on reimbursement.

Auditing and Monitoring in the Nonacute Setting

In nonacute care settings, such as nursing facilities or home health, health record documentation should be monitored to ensure that it is in accordance with applicable regulatory requirements and supports the claims submitted. In nursing facilities, MDS data should be periodically reviewed to ensure accuracy, the presence of supporting health record documentation, and inter-rater reliability. Computer edits should be put in place to ensure the electronic submission of error-free, complete, and consistent MDS data. Examples of basic edit checks include verification that responses are within range, the assessment is complete, responses are clinically consistent, and data are accurate. Periodic reviews (according to the facility's established evaluation and audit schedule) to compare the MDS, claim form, and health record documentation should be conducted. In the home health setting, similar auditing and monitoring processes should be implemented to ensure the accuracy of the OASIS data and the presence of supporting health record documentation. For reimbursement under a PPS, health record documentation and the assigned reimbursement category (such as RUG, DRG, or HHRG) should be regularly monitored to ensure accuracy and consistency.

Insufficient Coding Skills as Compliance Risk

Lack of sufficient coding skills to ensure accurate ICD-9-CM coding is a compliance risk in all healthcare settings. Personnel responsible for assignment of the ICD-9-CM codes should have the following:

- A knowledge of anatomy and physiology, disease processes, pharmacology, medical terminology

- An understanding of the content of the health record and knowledge of documentation requirements

- A knowledge of and an ability to apply coding rules and conventions, the *Official ICD-9-CM Guidelines for Coding and Reporting,* and reimbursement policies and regulations

- Ongoing continuing education in coding to keep skills up-to-date

It may be necessary to require coding personnel to complete a formal coding program and/or obtain coding certification (see page 36 for the subsection titled Qualifications for Coding Positions).

CMS's Payment Error Prevention Program

A 1998 audit of Medicare payments conducted by the OIG revealed that approximately $12.5 billion in improper payments were made and approximately 25 percent of those payments were for inpatient PPS services. In response, CMS has launched a major initiative to protect Medicare funds and significantly reduce the level of improper Medicare payments.

The Payment Error Prevention Program (PEPP) is an important part of this effort and is a national, three-year initiative aimed at reducing the overall Medicare PPS inpatient hospital payment error rate by monitoring inpatient hospital PPS claims and educating providers regarding payment errors. PEPP is administered and overseen by the quality improvement organizations (QIOs, formerly peer review organizations [PROs]) as part of their Sixth Scope of Work. As part of CMS's Health Care Quality Improvement Program, QIOs have been responsible for collaborating with hospitals and physicians to improve quality of care. PEPP represents an expansion of these collaborative efforts to include improvement of hospital structures and processes that contribute to payment errors. Under PEPP, QIOs are required to identify the following:

- Trends or patterns suggestive of incorrect DRG assignment

- Medically unnecessary admissions

- Insufficient documentation

- Inappropriate, unreasonable or medically unnecessary care

- Inappropriate transfers

- Premature discharges

Once suspected payment errors have been identified through data analysis, a focused review is conducted.

Each QIO has the autonomy and ability to identify the problem areas in its state and how best to solve them. PEPP is designed to be educational, rather than punitive, in nature. Whenever a confirmed pattern of errors is identified through focused review, the hospital is asked to develop a corrective action plan to resolve the problem. The success of the hospital's intervention is monitored through ongoing analysis of quarterly profiles and/or additional focused review. It is important to note that the QIOs are examining the quality of the physician documentation to support the diagnosis and procedure codes as well as the actual accuracy of the coding. The QIOs will also work to reduce payment errors by implementing payment error prevention projects that include intervention impacting all hospitals, such as providing education on specific topics. Intervention successes and lessons learned through QIO/hospital collaborative projects will be shared between QIOs via a management information system to encourage similar improvements nationwide. Each QIO will be evaluated with regard to its PEPP activities and will be judged to be successful if it achieves at least a 10 percent relative reduction in the payment error rate, performs the required first-year projects within the agreed-upon time frames, conforms to all reporting requirements, and establishes contact and coordination with local, state, and federal agencies and Medicare contractors and pertinent law enforcement activities.

In order to be prepared for the impact of PEPP on their organizations, as well as be able to effectively collaborate with the QIOs on reduction of the Medicare payment error rate, HIM professionals should do the following:

- Become thoroughly knowledgeable about the specific components of the PEPP program being implemented by the local QIO

- Identify and correct coding errors through audits before the errors are identified by the QIO

- Evaluate the quality of physician documentation and work with the medical staff to make improvements in documentation where necessary

- Ensure that the coding staff is receiving regular, ongoing education to keep its skills up-to-date and that targeted education is provided to address knowledge deficiencies

- Ensure that the medical staff is receiving regular, ongoing education on proper documentation principles and that targeted training is provided to address identified patterns of documentation deficiencies

References

Abraham, Prinny Rose. 2001. Trends to watch in home health compliance. *Journal of the American Health Information Management Association* 72(5):47.

American Health Information Management Association. 2001. AHIMA Position Statement: Privacy Official. Available at www.ahima.org/infocenter/positions/PrivOffState2k1.htm.

Centers for Medicare and Medicaid Services. 2001 (September 26). ICD-9-CM coding for diagnostic tests. Program Memorandum Intermediaries/Carriers. Transmittal AB-01-144. Available at http://hcfa.gov/pubforms/transmit/AB01144.pdf.

General Accounting Office. 2001 (June). Health Care: Consultants' Billing Advice May Lead to Improperly Paid Insurance Claims. GAO-01-818. Available at www.gao.gov/new.items/d01818.pdf.

Hammen, Cheryl. 2001. Choosing consultants without compromising compliance. *Journal of the American Health Information Management Association* 72(9):26, 28, 30.

Help wanted: privacy officer. 2001. *Journal of the American Health Information Management Association* 72(6):37–39.

Office of Inspector General. 1998 (February 23). Publication of the OIG compliance program guidance for hospitals: notice. *Federal Register* 63(35):8987–98. Available at http://oig.hhs.gov/authorities/docs/cpghosp.pdf.

Office of Inspector General. 2000 (June 12). Draft OIG compliance program for individual and small group physician practices, *Federal Register* 65(113):36818–35.

Office of Inspector General. 2001a. HHS/OIG Fiscal Year 2001 Work Plan: Health Care Financing Administration. Available at http://oig.hhs.gov/reading/workplan/2001/hcfa.pdf.

Office of Inspector General. 2001b (June). Practices of Business Consultants. Available at http://oig.hhs.gov/fraud/docs/alertsandbulletins/consultants.pdf.

Russo, Ruthann. 1998. *Seven Steps to HIM Compliance.* Marblehead, Mass.: Opus Communications, Inc.

Scichilone, Rita. 2002. Best practices for medical necessity validation. *Journal of the American Health Information Management Association* 73(2):48, 50.

Skurka, Margaret A. 2001. Navigating the physician services maze. *Journal of the American Health Information Management Association* 72(7):51–58.

Stewart, Margaret Morgan. 2001. *Coding and Reimbursement under the Outpatient Prospective Payment System.* Chicago: American Health Information Management Association.

Appendix A
Health Information Management Skills Fundamental to Effective Compliance

The background of health information management (HIM) professionals is invaluable to the process of achieving effective compliance and reducing the risk of future fraudulent or abusive practices. HIM professionals have specialized education, training, and certification in the management of health information, and they are responsible for the achievement and maintenance of data of the highest quality. They are specialists in collecting, analyzing, processing, integrating, storing, and securing healthcare data. Their education includes extensive training in the classification and coding of healthcare information for reimbursement, statistical, and research purposes. Finally, they are responsible for translating clinical information into coded data and then evaluating, analyzing, and maintaining its accuracy, validity, and meaningfulness.

HIM professionals are employed in a variety of healthcare settings, including hospitals, clinics, mental health facilities, nursing homes, and physicians' offices, as well as payers, managed care organizations, government agencies, law firms, accounting firms, consulting firms, vendors of healthcare products and services, health data organizations, and educational institutions. They possess many skills that are critical to an effective compliance program, including:

- A strong knowledge base in complete and accurate clinical documentation in all healthcare settings and for all healthcare disciplines

- A strong knowledge base and experience in appropriate coding and billing practices

- Knowledge of the conventions, rules, and guidelines for multiple classification systems

- Knowledge of multiple reimbursement systems

- Knowledge of multiple regulations, standards, policies, and requirements pertaining to clinical documentation, coding, and billing

- Knowledge of multiple third-party payer requirements

- The ability to accurately interpret and implement regulatory standards
- The ability to interpret legal requirements
- An established rapport with physicians and other healthcare practitioners
- Strong managerial, leadership, and interpersonal skills
- Strong communication and presentation skills
- Strong analytical skills

The HIM profession has a long history of deep-rooted commitment to honesty, integrity, and professional ethics.

Appendix B
High-Risk Areas for Fraud/Abuse Enforcement

Risk Areas Targeted by the HHS Office of Inspector General

The following are risk areas identified in the Office of Inspector General (OIG) 2002 Work Plan. This is not an all-inclusive list.

Hospitals

- **One-day hospital stays:** This review will evaluate Controls designed to ensure the reasonableness of Medicare inpatient hospital payments for beneficiaries discharged after spending only one day in a hospital.

- **Hospital discharges and subsequent readmissions:** This series of reviews will examine Medicare claims for beneficiaries who were discharged and subsequently readmitted relatively soon to the same or another acute care prospective payment system hospital. With the assistance of the Centers for Medicare and Medicaid Services (CMS) medical review resources, the OIG will determine if these claims were appropriately paid. The OIG will also review claim processing procedures to determine the effectiveness of existing system edits used to identify and review diagnosis- and/or time-related admissions.

- **Consecutive inpatient stays:** The OIG will examine the extent to which Medicare beneficiaries receive acute and postacute care through sequential stays in different providers. This review will include an assessment of CMS instructions for identifying and evaluating consecutive beneficiary stays, including those in skilled nursing facilities, long-term care hospitals, and prospective payment system-exempt units.

- **Payments to acute care prospective payment system hospitals:** This review will examine diagnosis-related groups that have a history of abusive coding to determine whether some prospective payment system hospitals continue to exhibit aberrant coding patterns.

- **Diagnosis-related group payment limits:** The OIG will continue to assess the ability of Medicare contractors to limit payments to hospitals for patients who are discharged from a prospective payment system hospital and admitted to one of several post-acute-care settings.

- **Diagnosis-related group payment window—Part B providers:** This review will determine the extent of duplicate claims submitted by Part B providers for services, such as ambulance, laboratory, or x-ray services, provided to hospital inpatients.

- **Expansion of diagnosis-related group payment window:** The OIG will determine the extent of preadmission services rendered outside the current 72-hour diagnosis-related group payment window and the amount of savings that can be achieved by expanding the payment window.

- **Outpatient prospective payment system:** The OIG will continue to review the implementation of the new prospective payment system for care provided to Medicare beneficiaries by hospital outpatient departments. They will evaluate the effectiveness of internal controls intended to ensure that services are adequately documented, properly coded, and medically necessary. Controls over "pass-through" costs will also be reviewed.

- **Outpatient services on same day as discharge and readmission:** The OIG will review outpatient services provided on the same day that a beneficiary was discharged and readmitted to the same prospective payment system hospital. This review will determine whether beneficiaries were discharged from a prospective payment system hospital, transported to another prospective payment system hospital for outpatient services, and readmitted to the first hospital on the same day and the appropriateness of Medicare reimbursement for the outpatient services.

- **Procedure coding of outpatient and physician services:** The OIG will review the procedure coding of outpatient services billed by a hospital and a physician for the same service. In a previous review, they identified a twenty-three percent (23%) nationwide rate of inconsistency between hospital outpatient department procedure coding and physician procedure coding for the same outpatient service. This review will determine whether these coding differences continue and, if so, how they affect the Medicare program.

Physicians

- **Advance beneficiary notices:** The OIG will examine the use of advance notices to Medicare beneficiaries and their financial impact on beneficiaries and providers. Practices seem to vary widely regarding when advance beneficiary notices are provided, especially with respect to noncovered laboratory services.

- **Physicians at teaching hospitals:** This initiative is designed to verify compliance with Medicare rules governing payment for physician services provided in the teaching hospital setting and to ensure that claims accurately reflect the level of service provided to patients.

- **Physician evaluation and management codes:** The OIG will determine whether physicians correctly coded evaluation and management services in physician offices and effectively used documentation guidelines. They will also assess whether carriers identified any instances of incorrect coding and what corrective actions they took.

- **Consultations:** This study will determine the appropriateness of billings for physician consultation services and the financial impact on the Medicare program from any inaccurate billings.

- **Services and supplies incident to physicians' services:** The OIG will evaluate the conditions under which physicians bill "incident-to" services and supplies.

Nursing Home Care

- **Quality assessment and assurance committees:** The OIG will examine the role and effectiveness of quality assessment and assurance committees in ensuring quality of care in nursing homes.

- **Three-day stay requirement:** The OIG will follow up on the CMS response to the findings and recommendations of the OIG's prior review of patient eligibility for care in skilled nursing facilities. The OIG found that some Medicare patients were not eligible for such care because they had not received sufficient hospital/nursing home care before the skilled nursing care.

- **Consolidated billing requirements:** The OIG will monitor CMS's efforts to determine the extent of overpayments during Calendar Year 2000 for certain Part B services subject to the consolidated billing provisions of the prospective payment system for skilled nursing facilities. They will also monitor the success of CMS's collection of previously identified overpayments.

Home Health

- **Home health payment system controls:** The OIG will monitor implementation of the new prospective payment system used to pay home health agencies for providing care to Medicare beneficiaries. They will evaluate the adequacy of controls intended to ensure that services are provided only to homebound individuals and are adequately documented, properly coded, and medically necessary, as well as controls over advance payments to providers. They will also determine whether payments are appropriately based on the location where the service is provided (patient's home) rather than where the service is billed (typically the urban location of the parent home health agency).

- **Coding of home health resource groups:** This review will determine whether home health agencies classified their patients in the appropriate case-mix category. The OIG will assess whether home health agencies received higher payments than warranted due to miscoding.

Other Medicare Services

- **Medicare payments for clinical trials:** This study will determine whether Medicare payments associated with clinical trials were made in accordance with program requirements. The OIG will also assess program safeguards related to clinical trial claim processing requirements.

- **Medicare mental health national error rate:** The OIG will develop a national payment error rate for Medicare fee-for-service mental health claims. They will conduct medical reviews of a sample of claims to determine medical necessity, coding accuracy, coverage, and (for inpatient services) setting of care.

Medicaid

- **Mutually exclusive procedure codes:** The OIG will determine the extent of potential overpayments or savings that could accrue to the Federal and State governments under the Medicaid program if edits were implemented to identify and deny payments for procedure codes that CMS has identified as mutually exclusive. As part of the National Correct Coding Initiative, guidelines were established for billing a variety of services. While these guidelines include edits for mutually exclusive procedure codes, they are not mandated for use in the Medicaid program.

Investigations

- **Healthcare fraud:** The OIG will investigate individuals, facilities, or entities that bill the Medicare and/or Medicaid program for services not rendered, claims that manipulate payment codes in an effort to inflate reimbursement amounts, and other false claims submitted to obtain program funds. Special focus areas include pharmaceutical fraud and quality of care issues for beneficiaries residing in care facilities.

Other risk areas that have been identified by the OIG in its inspection and audit reports, fraud alerts, and compliance program guidance documents include:

- **Billing for items or services not actually rendered:** This practice involves submitting a claim representing that the provider performed a service, all or part of which was not performed.

- **Billing for items or services not actually documented:** This involves submitting a claim that can not be substantiated in the documentation.

- **Providing medically unnecessary services:** By law, no payment may be made under Medicare Part A or Part B for any expenses incurred for items or services that are not reasonable and necessary for the diagnosis or treatment of illness or injury or to improve the functioning of the malformed body member. A claim requesting payment for medically unnecessary services intentionally seeks reimbursement for a service that is not warranted by the patient's current and documented medical condition.

- **Local medical review policies:** An area of concern relating to determinations of reasonable and necessary services is the variation in local medical review policies (LMRPs) among carriers. Physician practices are to bill the federal health programs only for items and services that are covered. In order to determine if an item or service is covered for Medicare, physician practices must be knowledgeable of the LMRPs applicable to their practices' jurisdiction. When the LMRP indicates that an item or service may not be covered by Medicare, the physician practice is responsible to convey this information to the patient so that the patient can make an informed decision concerning the health care services he/she may want to receive. This information is conveyed through advance beneficiary notices.

- **Advance beneficiary notices:** The use of ABNs is an area where physician practices experience numerous difficulties. Practices can help to reduce problems in this area by educating their physicians on the correct use of ABNs, obtaining guidance from the carrier regarding their interpretation of whether an ABN is necessary where the service is not covered, developing a standard form for all diagnostic tests, and developing a process for handling patients who refuse to sign ABNs.

- **Billing for noncovered services as if covered:** Physicians sometimes submit claims for services in order to receive a denial from the carrier, thereby enabling the patient to submit the denied claim for payment to a secondary payer. In instances where a claim is being submitted to Medicare for this purpose, the physician should indicate on the claim that it is being submitted for the purpose of receiving a denial in order to bill a secondary insurance carrier. This step should assist carriers and prevent inadvertent payments to which the physician is not entitled. In some instances, however, the carrier pays the claim even though the service is noncovered and the physician did not intend for payment to be made. When this occurs, the physician has a responsibility to refund the amount paid and indicate that the service is not covered.

- **Duplicate billing:** This occurs when more than one claim is submitted for the same service or the bill is submitted to more than one primary payer at the same time. The OIG acknowledged that duplicate billing can occur due to simple errors, but that knowing duplicate billing, which is sometimes evidenced by systematic or repeated double billing, can create liability under criminal, civil, or administrative law, particularly if any overpayment is not promptly refunded.

- **Upcoding:** Upcoding is the practice of using a code that provides a higher payment rate than the code that actually reflects the service furnished to the patient.

- **DRG creep:** DRG creep is the practice of billing using a DRG that provides a higher payment rate than the DRG that accurately reflects the service furnished to the patient.

- **Unbundling:** Unbundling is the practice of submitting bills piecemeal or in fragmented fashion to maximize reimbursement for various tests or procedures that are required to be billed together and thus at a reduced cost.

- **Failure to properly use modifiers:** Since the use of CPT modifiers can determine whether a service is reimbursed or whether additional reimbursement is warranted, improper use of modifiers can result in inappropriate reimbursement.

- **Internal coding practices:** The OIG noted that internal coding practices, including software edits, should be reviewed periodicallly to determine consistency with all applicable federal, state, and private payer healthcare program requirements.

- **Assumption coding:** This refers to the coding of a diagnosis or procedure without supporting clinical documentation.

- **Clustering:** This refers to the practice of coding one or two middle levels of E/M codes exclusively, under the philosophy that some will be higher and some will be lower, and it will average out over time (in reality, this overcharges some patients while undercharging others).

- **Coding without proper documentation of all physician and other professional services:** The OIG noted that while proper documentation is the responsibility of the healthcare provider, the coding professional should be aware of proper documentation requirements and should encourage providers to document their services appropriately.

- **Lack of integrity in computer systems:** This involves the failure to have systems and processes in place to ensure the integrity of health information and that records can be easily located and accessed.

- **RUGS creep:** This is a risk created by the nursing facility PPS, in which there is an incentive to *overassess* residents in order to achieve higher payment rates.

- **Home health PPS:** Implementation of the home health PPS will require home health agencies to guard against new types of fraud, waste, and abuse. Potential risks include underutilization or overutilization, duplicate billing, and mischaracterization of the patient's condition. Payments based on episodes of care might create incentives to reduce the amount of services provided to patients or to characterize patients as sicker than they really are.

- **Third-party billing services:** Physicians should remember that they remain responsible to the Medicare program for bills sent in the physician's name or containing the physician's signature, even if the physician had no actual knowledge of a billing impropriety. It is no defense for the physician if the physician's billing service improperly bills Medicare. One of the most common risk areas involving billing services deals with physician practices contracting with billing services on a percentage basis. Although percentage-based billing arrangements are not illegal per se, the OIG has a longstanding concern that such arrangements may increase the risk of intentional upcoding and similar abusive billing practices.

- Alteration of documentation

- Unavailability of all necessary documentation at the time of coding

- Failure to maintain the confidentiality of information/records

- Computer software programs that encourage billing personnel to enter data in fields indicating services were rendered though not actually performed or documented

- Overutilization (furnishing more services than medically necessary) and underutilization (knowingly denying needed care in order to keep costs low)

- False dating of amendments to nursing notes

- Falsified plans of care

- Untimely and/or forged physician certification on plans of care

- Falsifying information on claim form, certificate of medical necessity, and/or accompanying documentation

- Providing misleading information about resident's medical condition on MDS or otherwise providing inaccurate information used to determine RUG assigned to resident

- Failure to comply with applicable requirements for verbal orders for hospice services

High-Risk DRGs Identified by Healthcare Industry Experts

The common reasons or contributing factors given for misclassification to these DRGs are not intended to be all-inclusive.

- **DRG 14, Specific cerebrovascular disorders except transient ischemic attack:** Some cases may more appropriately be classified to DRG 15 (Transient Ischemic Attack and Precerebral Occlusions). For example, the neurologic deficits may have been transient in nature. The physician documentation may be ambiguous as to whether the patient experienced a CVA or a TIA. The coding professional may have coded a CVA from a radiology report without supporting documentation from the attending physician. There are also variable interpretations as to the meaning of the fifth digits for categories 433 and 434, which may result in misclassification of some cases to DRG 14.

- **DRG 16, Nonspecific cerebrovascular disorders with CC:** Acute cerebro-vascular insufficiency, without further specification, is classified to this DRG. However, if the physician has documented that the acute cerebrovascular insufficiency has transient focal neurological signs and symptoms, the code for transient ischemic attack should be assigned instead, resulting in classification to DRG 15.

- **DRG 79, Respiratory infections and inflammations, age >17 with CC:** Specific type of pneumonia may be presumed, causal organism may be picked up from culture reports without supporting documentation from the attending physician, or pneumonia documented as due to multiple specified organisms may be inappropriately coded as "mixed" bacterial pneumonia.

- **DRG 87, Pulmonary edema and respiratory failure:** Misapplication of coding guidelines for respiratory failure may result in incorrect classification of cases to this DRG. Clinical findings (such as arterial blood gases) may be used to justify reporting a principal diagnosis of respiratory failure without supporting documentation from the attending physician. Respiratory failure may inappropriately be sequenced as the principal diagnosis when another diagnosis, such as myocardial infarction, congestive heart failure, chronic obstructive pulmonary disease, or cerebrovascular accident, more appropriately meets the definition of principal diagnosis. Pulmonary edema may be inappropriately coded separately from congestive heart failure.

- **DRG 88, Chronic obstructive pulmonary disease:** If asthma and bronchitis are incorrectly coded as "chronic obstructive," the case will be classified to this DRG instead of DRG 96 or 97.

- **DRG 89, Simple pneumonia and pleurisy, age >17 with CC:** Pneumonia may be reported as the principal diagnosis, but the medical record documentation only supports a diagnosis of bronchitis.

- **DRG 121, Circulatory disorders with acute myocardial infarction and major complications, discharged alive:** A major complication may be coded without supporting physician documentation. If there is no major complication, the case is classified to DRG 122. If an acute myocardial infarction is incorrectly coded, DRG misclassification will also occur.

- **DRG 124, Circulatory disorders except acute myocardial infarction with cardiac catheterization and complex diagnosis:** A complex diagnosis may be coded without supporting physician documentation. Cases without a complex diagnosis are classified to DRG 125.

- **DRG 127, Heart failure and shock:** Congestive heart failure may be inappropriately sequenced as the principal diagnosis instead of angina.

- **DRG 130, Peripheral vascular disorders with CC:** Thrombophlebitis of the lower extremities may inappropriately be coded as thrombophlebitis of the superficial vessels without supporting physician documentation. Thrombophlebitis of the superficial vessels of the lower extremities is classified to DRG 130, but unspecified thrombophlebitis or that of deep vessels is classified to DRG 128.

- **DRG 132, Atherosclerosis with CC:** Arteriosclerotic heart disease may be inappropriately sequenced as the principal diagnosis instead of angina. If the physician documents that the angina is due to arteriosclerotic heart disease, or links them, the arteriosclerotic heart disease should be sequenced first. However, if the physician does not link the two conditions, angina should be sequenced as the principal diagnosis.

- **DRG 138, Cardiac arrhythmia and conduction disorders with CC:** Cardiac arrhythmia may be inappropriately sequenced as the principal diagnosis instead of angina.

- **DRG 140, Angina pectoris:** Chest pain may be inappropriately coded as angina without supporting physician documentation.

- **DRG 144, Other circulatory system diagnoses with CC:** A common problem resulting in misclassification to this DRG is determination of whether the appropriate principal diagnosis is a subsequent episode of care for a myocardial infarction (within the applicable eight-week time frame), arteriosclerotic heart disease, chest pain, or angina.

- **DRG 174, Gastrointestinal hemorrhage with CC:** Gastrointestinal disorders, such as diverticulitis or gastritis, may inappropriately be coded as that with hemorrhage instead of without hemorrhage. Physician documentation linking the patient's bleeding with the identified gastrointestinal disorder is necessary in order to assign the fifth digit for "with hemorrhage."

- **DRG 188, Other digestive system diagnoses, age >17 with CC:** Classification to the appropriate digestive system DRG depends on clear documentation of the digestive system symptom or definitive diagnosis necessitating admission. For example, abdominal pain is classified to DRG 182, whereas abdominal rigidity is classified to DRG 188. Diaphragmatic hernia is classified to DRG 182, whereas other types of hernia are classified to DRG 188. Toxic gastroenteritis and colitis and that due to radiation are classified to DRG 188, whereas other types of gastroenteritis and colitis are classified to DRG 182. Also, a digestive disorder classified to DRG 188 may be inappropriately sequenced as the principal diagnosis instead of gastrointestinal obstruction.

- **DRG 239, Pathological fractures and musculoskeletal and connective tissue malignancy:** Misclassification to this DRG can occur when pathological fracture is inappropriately sequenced as the principal diagnosis, but the correct principal diagnosis is a traumatic fracture or osteoporosis.

- **DRG 296, Nutritional and miscellaneous metabolic disorders, age >17 with CC:** Some cases may more appropriately be classified to DRG 182, Esophagitis, gastroenteritis, and miscellaneous digestive disorders, age >17 with CC. A key issue is whether the patient was admitted for dehydration or the underlying gastrointestinal disorder. Or, an underlying urinary tract infection may be the appropriate principal diagnosis rather than dehydration.

- **DRG 316, Renal failure:** Renal failure may be inappropriately sequenced as the principal diagnosis instead of dehydration. If dehydration is sequenced as the principal diagnosis, the case is classified to either DRG 296 or 297 (depending on whether there is a CC or not). Also, renal failure may be inappropriately sequenced as the principal diagnosis instead of the underlying renal disease.

- **DRG 416, Septicemia, age >17:** Some cases may more appropriately be classified to DRGs 320 or 321. The key issue is whether the patient has septicemia or a urinary tract infection. The confusion typically results from physician documentation of the term "urosepsis."

- **DRG 429, Organic disturbances and mental retardation:** When psychosis is inappropriately coded as a "senile" condition, it is classified to this DRG instead of DRG 430.

- **DRG 475, Respiratory system diagnosis with ventilator support:** A common reason for misclassification of cases to this DRG is whether the patient's principal diagnosis is respiratory or not. Patients with a respiratory principal diagnosis on mechanical ventilation are classified to DRG 475, but those with a non-respiratory principal diagnosis are not classified to this DRG. A respiratory diagnosis may inappropriately be sequenced as the principal diagnosis in order to classify the patient to DRG 475. For example, when respiratory failure is due to congestive heart failure, the congestive heart failure should be sequenced as the principal diagnosis, which would cause the case to be classified to a different, lower-weighted DRG. Other factors resulting in cases being misclassified to DRG 475 include: unclear physician documentation as to the etiology of the respiratory failure; incorrect coding of BIPAP (bi-level positive airway pressure) or CPAP (continuous positive airway pressure) as continuous mechanical ventilation; and continuous mechanical ventilation was coded, but ventilator was only used during surgery.

Source: HHS/OIG Fiscal Year 2002 Work Plan: Centers for Medicare and Medicaid Services.

Appendix C
Sample Tools for Implementation of an HIM Compliance Program

Sample Outlines for Internal Educational Programs

Sample Communication Tools for Improving Physician Documentation

Sample Job Description for HIM Compliance Specialist

HIM Compliance Checklist

Sample Outlines for Internal Educational Programs

Following are suggested agenda items for educational programs on HIM compliance issues aimed at different target audiences. The programs may be presented by the HIM compliance specialist or another designated HIM representative. Each organization should customize its educational programs to meet its own needs. The specific information to be covered on each subject would be at the discretion of the presenter. Additional topics should be included, as appropriate. Pertinent elements of the organization's HIM compliance program should be covered in educational programs, as appropriate for the particular audience. It would be helpful to include a few examples or to provide case scenarios that fit the audience. Educational programs should be interactive in order to demonstrate the participants' understanding of the material presented.

Admitting Department

- Background of fraud and abuse enforcement
- OIG target areas
- Accurate and complete diagnosis
- Relationship to HIM and coding
- Medical necessity issues
- Data quality (including overview of key coding rules and guidelines)
- Future payment methodologies (for example, impact of outpatient PPS)
- Pertinent review and audit results (positive and negative)
- Pertinent payer-specific policies
- HIM role in systemwide compliance (Where does HIM fit in?)
- Input from participants on process improvements (for example, suggestions from participants regarding ways to streamline operations or improve documentation to ensure compliance)

- Designing educational programs for admitting staff (that is, suggested topics for ongoing educational initiatives and areas that should be covered in new employee training)

Ancillary Services (Nursing, Lab, Radiology, Dietary, Physical Medicine, and So On)

- Background of fraud and abuse enforcement
- OIG target areas
- Accurate and complete documentation
- Relationship of documentation and coding
- Skills necessary for accurate coding
- Medical necessity issues
- Chargemaster maintenance
- Regulatory requirements pertaining to coding and documentation
- Pertinent payer-specific policies
- New coding requirements (for example, new ICD-9-CM or CPT codes affecting ancillary services)
- Data quality
- Future payment methodologies
- Pertinent audit results (positive and negative)
- HIM role in systemwide compliance (Where does HIM fit in?)
- Input from participants on process improvements
- Designing educational programs for ancillary services (initial and ongoing)

Business Office Services

- Background of fraud and abuse enforcement
- OIG target areas
- Relationship of documentation and coding
- Coding process
- Skills necessary for accurate coding
- Relationship between coding and billing functions
- Role of coding in resolution of claims rejections
- Medical necessity issues
- Chargemaster maintenance
- Coding and billing compliance
- Communication with payers (for example, documentation of payer advice)

- Communication of payer memos or bulletins to all affected departments
- Pertinent payer-specific policies
- Data quality
- Future payment methodologies (for example, impact of outpatient PPS)
- HIM role in systemwide compliance (Where does HIM fit in?)
- Input from participants on process improvements
- Designing educational programs for business office personnel (initial and ongoing)

Administration

- Background of fraud and abuse enforcement
- OIG target areas
- Consequences of noncompliance
- Linkage of documentation and coding to compliance
- OIG model compliance programs
- Compliance and the medical staff
- HIM recommendations for process improvements (for example, suggestions based on risk assessment or audit results)
- Future payment methodologies (for example, impact of outpatient PPS)
- HIM as a vital link to systemwide compliance (Where does HIM fit in?)

Medical Staff

- Background of fraud and abuse enforcement
- OIG target areas
- Complete and accurate documentation practices
- Relationship of documentation and coding
- Pertinent payer-specific policies
- Medical necessity issues
- Data quality
- Future payment methodologies
- Pertinent review and audit results (positive and negative)
- Designing review programs and audits for physician practices (prospective versus retrospective)
- HIM role in systemwide compliance (Where does HIM fit in?)
- Understanding the physician's role in compliance
- Input from participants on process improvements

Sample Communication Tools for Improving Physician Documentation

The following are sample forms to be used to provide guidance to physicians regarding appropriate documentation of history and physicals, discharge summaries, operative reports, and consultations. Each healthcare organization should design its own tool(s) to assist in communicating regulatory requirements on documentation (JCAHO, CMS, and so on) to physicians. Common documentation deficiencies identified by the organization may be incorporated.

History and Physicals

Date:

To: *[Insert medical staff or specific physician name]*

From: *[Insert HIM director name, title, and telephone number]*

Re: Health Record Documentation Requirements

The following information is provided to assist and guide you in proper health record documentation compliance. Increasing scrutiny is being directed toward complete and accurate physician documentation.

All dictated reports *must* include:

- Patient name
- Health record number
- Date of admission, consult, operation, and so on
- List of physicians for sending copies
- Type of report

To determine medical necessity and ensure proper coding and billing, the following elements are recommended for history and physical reports:

- Chief complaint, admitting diagnosis
- Present illness
- Past history (including allergies, current medication, and conditions)
- Family history and social history
- Review of systems
- Physical exam (*must include* pelvic, breast, and rectal exams or *reason why deferred*)
- Diabetic patient (fundoscopic eye examination and peripheral pulses)
- Treatment plan (plan of care)
- Impression

For preoperative history and physicals, a statement regarding the risks, benefits, options, and potential complications of the procedure, as well as blood transfusion, if applicable, should be included. This is required in some states.

Discharge Summaries

Date:

To: *[Insert medical staff or specific physician name]*

From: *[Insert HIM director name, title, and telephone number]*

Re: Health Record Documentation Requirements

The following information is provided to assist and guide you in proper health record documentation compliance. Increasing scrutiny is being directed toward complete and accurate physician documentation.

All dictated reports must include:

- Patient name
- Health record number
- Date of admission, consult, operation, and so on
- List of physicians for sending copies
- Type of report

To determine medical necessity and ensure proper coding and billing, the following elements are recommended for discharge summaries:

- Date of admission/date of discharge
- Admitting diagnosis and history
- Significant findings
- Hospital course (including procedures performed and treatment rendered)
- Complications
- Discharge instructions (including activity, diet, and medications)
- Condition on discharge
- Disposition (if transferred, state what level of care the receiving facility will provide [rehab, acute care, and so on])
- Principal diagnosis (condition found after study to be chiefly responsible for admission)
- Additional diagnoses (those conditions identified, evaluated, treated, or that required additional resources or extended the length of stay)
  —Comorbid conditions (COPD, CHF, diabetes, and so on)
  —Complications
- Plan for follow-up care

Operative Reports

Date:

To: *[Insert medical staff or specific physician name]*

From: *[Insert HIM director name, title, and telephone number]*

Re: Health Record Documentation Requirements

The following information is provided to assist and guide you in proper health record documentation compliance. Increasing scrutiny is being directed toward complete and accurate physician documentation.

All dictated reports must include:

- Patient name
- Health record number
- Date of admission, consult, operation, and so on
- List of physicians for sending copies
- Type of report

To determine medical necessity and ensure proper coding and billing, the following elements are recommended for operative reports:

- Preoperative diagnosis
- Postoperative diagnosis
- Operation(s)/procedure(s) performed (do not use abbreviations)
- Indications
- Surgeon
- Assistant surgeon
- Anesthesiologist
- Type of anesthesia
- Findings
- Description of procedure
- Specimens removed
- Sutures/drains
- Estimated blood loss
- Fluids replaced (for example, blood transfusions)
- Complications (describe)
- Disposition (condition at conclusion of procedure)

Consultations

Date:

To: *[Insert medical staff or specific physician name]*

From: *[Insert HIM director name, title, and telephone number]*

Re: Health Record Documentation Requirements

The following information is provided to assist and guide you in proper health record documentation compliance. Increasing scrutiny is being directed toward complete and accurate physician documentation.

All dictated reports must include:

- Patient name
- Health record number
- Date of admission, consult, operation, and so on
- List of physicians for sending copies
- Type of report

To determine medical necessity and ensure proper coding and billing, the following elements are recommended for consultation reports:

- Reason for consultation or evaluation
- Requesting physician
- Current history
- Past medical history
- Physical exam and review of systems (may be limited depending on circumstances)
- Pertinent laboratory/radiology findings and/or studies
- Treatment plan
- Impression/conclusion

Sample Job Description for HIM Compliance Specialist

Title: HIM Compliance Specialist   **Reports to:** Corporate Compliance Officer

Qualifications:

- RHIA or RHIT
- CCS preferred (or CCS-P for professional services coding)
- Extensive knowledge of ICD-9-CM and CPT coding principles and guidelines
- Extensive knowledge of reimbursement systems
- Extensive knowledge of proper use of HCPCS codes
- Chargemaster experience
- Extensive knowledge of federal, state, and payer-specific regulations and policies pertaining to documentation, coding, and billing
- Understanding of relationship among coding, billing, and reimbursement
- Experience with reviewing and analyzing claims, denials, and rejections
- Five years of hospital coding experience (for ambulatory services, ambulatory coding experience)
- Strong managerial, leadership, and interpersonal skills
- Excellent written and oral communication skills
- Excellent analytical skills

Responsibilities:

- Oversees and monitors implementation of the HIM compliance program
- Develops and coordinates educational and training programs regarding elements of the HIM compliance program, such as appropriate documentation and accurate coding, to all appropriate personnel, including HIM coding staff, physicians, billing personnel, and ancillary departments

- Maintains attendance rosters and documentation (agenda, handouts, and so on) for HIM training programs

- Ensures that coding consultants and other contracted entities (for example, out-sourced coding personnel) understand and agree to adhere to the organization's HIM compliance program

- Conducts regular audits and coordinates ongoing monitoring of coding accuracy and documentation adequacy

- Provides feedback and focused educational programs on the results of auditing and monitoring activities to affected staff and physicians

- Conducts trend analyses to identify patterns and variations in coding practices and case-mix index

- Compares coding and reimbursement profile with national and regional norms to identify variations requiring further investigation

- Reviews claim denials and rejections pertaining to coding and medical necessity issues and, when necessary, implements corrective action plan, such as educational programs, to prevent similar denials and rejections from recurring

- Conducts internal investigations of changes in coding practices or reports of other potential problems pertaining to coding

- Initiates corrective action to ensure resolution of problem areas identified during an internal investigation or auditing/monitoring activity

- Reports noncompliance issues detected through auditing and monitoring, nature of corrective action plans implemented in response to identified problems, and results of follow-up audits to the corporate compliance officer

- Receives and investigates reports of HIM compliance violations and communicates this information to the corporate compliance officer

- Recommends disciplinary action for violation of the compliance program, the organization's standards of conduct, or coding policies and procedures to the corporate compliance officer

- Ensures the appropriate dissemination and communication of all regulation, policy, and guideline changes to affected personnel

- Serves as a resource for department managers, staff, physicians, and administration to obtain information or clarification on accurate and ethical coding and documentation standards, guidelines, and regulatory requirements

- Monitors adherence to the HIM compliance program

- Revises the HIM compliance program in response to changing organizational needs or new or revised regulations, policies, and guidelines

- Serves on the compliance committee

- Recommends revisions to the corporate compliance program to improve its effectiveness

HIM Compliance Checklist

☐ Has an HIM code of conduct been developed and signed by HIM staff?

☐ Has an individual been designated to oversee the HIM compliance program?

☐ Has an internal risk assessment been conducted?

☐ Have comprehensive coding and documentation policies and procedures been developed and/or revised?

☐ Have educational programs been designed to ensure that staff and physicians are receiving adequate training on the elements of the compliance program, with particular emphasis on coding and documentation requirements?

☐ Do job descriptions for coding positions accurately reflect the necessary qualifications for these positions?

☐ Have processes been established for reporting, investigating, correcting, and following up on compliance-related violations?

☐ Have mechanisms for reporting compliance-related issues been communicated to employees, physicians, and contractors?

☐ Has a mechanism been established for employees, physicians, and contractors to obtain clarification on a policy, procedure, or element of the compliance program (including answers to billing and coding questions)?

☐ Is there a centralized source and systematic process for disseminating statutory and regulatory information in a timely fashion?

☐ Have processes been put in place for regular auditing and monitoring of coding accuracy and for addressing any identified problems?

☐ Have processes been established to investigate variations or other problems identified through auditing and monitoring such that the cause, scope, and seriousness of the problem can reasonably be determined and appropriate corrective action initiated?

☐ Has an action plan for responding to state or federal investigations been developed and approved?

☐ Has compliance been incorporated into the staff performance evaluation process?

☐ Have the various levels of disciplinary action that may be imposed for failure to comply been communicated to all affected individuals?

Appendix D
AHIMA Positions and Practice Guidelines

AHIMA Practice Brief: Developing a Physician Query Process

AHIMA Practice Brief: Developing a Coding Compliance Policy Document

American Health Information Management (AHIMA) Statement on Consistency of Healthcare Diagnostic and Procedural Coding

AHIMA Position Statement: Quality Healthcare Data and Information

AHIMA Practice Brief: Data Quality

AHIMA Resolution: Advocating for Quality Documentation and Adherence to Official Coding Guidelines

AHIMA Practice Brief: Developing a Physician Query Process

Principles of Medical Record Documentation

Medical record documentation is used for a multitude of purposes, including:

- Serving as a means of communication between the physician and the other members of the healthcare team providing care to the patient

- Serving as a basis for evaluating the adequacy and appropriateness of patient care

- Providing data to support insurance claims

- Assisting in protecting the legal interests of patients, healthcare professionals, and healthcare facilities

- Providing clinical data for research and education

To support these various uses, it is imperative that medical record documentation be complete, accurate, and timely. Facilities are expected to comply with a number of standards regarding medical record completion and content promulgated by multiple regulatory agencies.

Joint Commission on Accreditation of Healthcare Organizations

The Joint Commission's *2000 Hospital Accreditation Standards* state, "the medical record contains sufficient information to identify the patient, support the diagnosis, justify the treatment, document the course and results, and promote continuity among health care providers" (IM.7.2).[1] The Joint Commission Standards also state, "medical record data and information are managed in a timely manner" (IM.7.6).

Timely entries are essential if a medical record is to be useful in a patient's care. A complete medical record is also important when a patient is discharged, because information in the record may be needed for clinical, legal, or performance improvement purposes. The Joint Commission requires hospitals to have policy and procedures on the timely entry of all significant clinical information into the patient's medical record, and they do not consider a medical record complete until all final diagnoses and complications are recorded without the use of symbols or abbreviations.

Joint Commission standards also require medical records to be reviewed on an ongoing basis for completeness of timeliness of information, and action is taken to improve the quality and timeliness of documentation that affects patient care (IM.7.10). This review must address the presence, timeliness, legibility, and authentication of the final diagnoses and conclusions at termination of hospitalization.

Medicare

The Medicare Conditions of Participation require medical records to be accurately written, promptly completed, properly filed and retained, and accessible.[2] Records must document, as appropriate, complications, hospital-acquired infections, and unfavorable reactions to drugs and anesthesia. The conditions also stipulate that all records must document the final diagnosis with completion of medical records within 30 days following discharge.

Relationship between Coding and Documentation

Complete and accurate diagnostic and procedural coded data must be available, in a timely manner, in order to:

- Improve the quality and effectiveness of patient care

- Ensure equitable healthcare reimbursement

- Expand the body of medical knowledge

- Make appropriate decisions regarding healthcare policies, delivery systems, funding, expansion, and education

- Monitor resource utilization

- Permit identification and resolution of medical errors

- Improve clinical decision making

- Facilitate tracking of fraud and abuse

- Permit valid clinical research, epidemiological studies, outcomes and statistical analyses, and provider profiling

- Provide comparative data to consumers regarding costs and outcomes, average charges, and outcomes by procedure

Physician documentation is the cornerstone of accurate coding. Therefore, assuring the accuracy of coded data is a shared responsibility between coding professionals and physicians. Accurate diagnostic and procedural coded data originate from collaboration between physicians, who have a clinical background, and coding professionals, who have an understanding of classification systems.

Expectations of Physicians

Physicians are expected to provide complete, accurate, timely, and legible documentation of pertinent facts and observations about an individual's health history, including past and present illnesses, tests, treatments, and outcomes. Medical record entries should be documented at the time service is provided. Medical record entries should be authenticated. If subsequent additions to documentation are needed, they should be identified as such and dated. (Often these expectations are included in the medical staff or house staff rules and regulations.) Medical record documentation should:

- Address the clinical significance of abnormal test results

- Support the intensity of patient evaluation and treatment and describe the thought processes and complexity of decision making

- Include all diagnostic and therapeutic procedures, treatments, and tests performed, in addition to their results

- Include any changes in the patient's condition, including psychosocial and physical symptoms

- Include all conditions that coexist at the time of admission, that subsequently develop, or that affect the treatment received and the length of stay. This encompasses all conditions that affect patient care in terms of requiring clinical evaluation, therapeutic treatment, diagnostic procedures, extended length of hospital stay, or increased nursing care and monitoring[3]

- Be updated as necessary to reflect all diagnoses relevant to the care or services provided

- Be consistent and discuss and reconcile any discrepancies (this reconciliation should be documented in the medical record)

- Be legible and written in ink, typewritten, or electronically signed, stored, and printed

Expectations of Coding Professionals

The AHIMA Code of Ethics sets forth ethical principles for the HIM profession. HIM professionals are responsible for maintaining and promoting ethical practices. This Code of Ethics states, in part: "Health information management professionals promote high standards for health information management practice, education, and research."

Another standard in this code states, "Health information management professionals strive to provide accurate and timely information." Data accuracy and integrity are fundamental values of HIM that are advanced by:

- Employing practices that produce complete, accurate, and timely information to meet the health and related needs of individuals

- Following the guidelines set forth in the organization's compliance plan for reporting improper preparation, alteration, or suppression of information or data by others

- Not participating in any improper preparation, alteration, or suppression of health record information or other organization data

A conscientious goal for coding and maintaining a quality database is accurate clinical and statistical data. AHIMA's Standards of Ethical Coding were developed to guide coding professionals in this process. As stated in the standards, coding professionals are expected to support the importance of accurate, complete, and consistent coding practices for the production of quality healthcare data. These standards also indicate that coding professionals should only assign and report codes that are clearly and consistently supported by physician documentation in the medical record. It is the responsibility of coding professionals to assess physician documentation to assure that it supports the diagnosis and procedure codes reported on claims.

Dialogue between coding professionals and clinicians is encouraged, because it improves coding professionals' clinical knowledge and educates the physicians on documentation practice issues. AHIMA's Standards of Ethical Coding state that coding professionals are expected to consult physicians for clarification and additional documentation prior to code assignment when there is conflicting or ambiguous data in the health record. Coding professionals should also assist and educate physicians by advocating proper documentation practices, further specificity, and resequencing or inclusion of diagnoses or procedures when needed to more accurately reflect the acuity, severity, and the occurrence of events. It is recommended that coding be performed by credentialed HIM professionals.[4]

It is inappropriate for coding professionals to misrepresent the patient's clinical picture through incorrect coding or add diagnoses or procedures unsupported by the documentation to maximize reimbursement or meet insurance policy coverage requirements. Coding professionals should not change codes or the narratives of codes on the billing abstract so that meanings are misrepresented. Diagnoses or procedures should not be inappropriately included or excluded, because payment or insurance policy coverage requirements will be affected. When individual payer policies conflict with official coding rules and guidelines, these policies should be obtained in writing whenever possible. Reasonable efforts should be made to educate the payer on proper coding practices in order to influence a change in the payer's policy.

Proper Use of Physician Queries

The process of querying physicians is an effective and, in today's healthcare environment, necessary mechanism for improving the quality of coding and medical record documentation and capturing complete clinical data. Query forms have become an accepted tool for communicating with physicians on documentation issues influencing proper code assignment. Query forms should be used in a judicious and appropriate manner. They must be used as a communication tool to improve the accuracy of code assignment and the quality of physician documentation, not to inappropriately maximize reimbursement. The query process should be guided by AHIMA's Standards of Ethical Coding and the official coding guidelines. An inappropriate query—such as a form that is poorly constructed or asks leading questions—or overuse of the query process can result in quality-of-care, legal, and ethical concerns.

The Query Process

The goal of the query process should be to improve physician documentation and coding professionals' understanding of the unique clinical situation, not to improve reimbursement. Each facility should establish a policy and procedure for obtaining physician clarification of documentation that affects code assignment. The process of querying physicians must be a patient-specific process, not a general process. Asking "blanket" questions is not appropriate. Policies regarding the circumstances when physicians will be queried should be designed to promote timely, complete, and accurate coding and documentation.

Physicians should not be asked to provide clarification of their medical record documentation without the opportunity to access the patient's medical record.

Each facility also needs to determine if physicians will be queried concurrently (during the patient's hospitalization) or after discharge. Both methods are acceptable. Querying physicians concurrently allows the documentation deficiency to be corrected while the patient is still in-house and can positively influence patient care.

The policy and procedure should stipulate who is authorized to contact the physician for clarifications regarding a coding issue. Coding professionals should be allowed to contact physicians directly for clarification, rather than limiting this responsibility to supervisory personnel or a designated individual.

The facility may wish to use a designated physician liaison to resolve conflicts between physicians and coding professionals. The appropriate use of the physician liaison should be described in the facility's policy and procedures.

Query Format

Each facility should develop a standard format for the query form. No "sticky notes" or scratch paper should be allowed. Each facility should develop a standard design and format for physician queries to ensure clear, consistent, appropriate queries.

The query form should:

- Be clearly and concisely written

- Contain precise language

- Present the facts from the medical record and identify why clarification is needed

- Present the scenario and state a question that asks the physician to make a clinical interpretation of a given diagnosis or condition based on treatment, evaluation, monitoring, and/or services provided. "Open-ended" questions that allow the physician to document the specific diagnosis are preferable to multiple-choice questions or questions requiring only a "yes" or "no" response. Queries that appear to lead the physician to provide a particular response could lead to allegations of inappropriate upcoding

- Be phrased such that the physician is allowed to specify the correct diagnosis. It should not indicate the financial impact of the response to the query. The form should not be designed so that all that is required is a physician signature

- Include:

  —Patient name

  —Admission date

  —Medical record number

  —Name and contact information (phone number and e-mail address) of the coding professional

  —Specific question and rationale (that is, relevant documentation or clinical findings)

  —Place for physician to document his or her response

  —Place for the physician to sign and date his or her response

The query forms should not:

- "Lead" the physician

- Sound presumptive, directing, prodding, probing, or as though the physician is being led to make an assumption

- Ask questions that can be responded to in a "yes" or "no" fashion

- Indicate the financial impact of the response to the query

- Be designed so that all that is required is a physician signature

When Is a Query Appropriate?

Physicians should be queried whenever there is conflicting, ambiguous, or incomplete information in the medical record regarding any significant reportable condition or procedure. Querying the physician only when reimbursement is affected will skew national healthcare data and might lead to allegations of upcoding.

Every discrepancy or issue not addressed in the physician documentation should not necessarily result in the physician being queried. Each facility needs to develop policies and procedures regarding the clinical conditions and documentation situations warranting a request for physician clarification. For example, insignificant or irrelevant findings may not warrant querying the physician regarding the assignment of an additional diagnosis code. Also, if the maximum number of codes that can be entered in the hospital information system has already been assigned, the facility may decide that it is not necessary to query the physician regarding an additional code. Facilities need to balance the value of marginal data being collected against the administrative burden of obtaining the additional documentation.

Members of the medical staff in consultation with coding professionals should develop the specific clinical criteria for a valid query. The specific clinical documentation that must be present in the patient's record to generate a query should be described. For example, anemia, septicemia, and respiratory failure are conditions that often require physician clarification. The medical staff can assist the coding staff in determining when it would be appropriate to query a physician regarding the reporting of these conditions by describing the specific clinical indications in the medical record documentation that raise the possibility that the condition in question may be present.

When Is a Query Not Necessary?

Queries are not necessary if a physician involved in the care and treatment of the patient, including consulting physicians, has documented a diagnosis and there is no conflicting documentation from another physician. Medical record documentation from any physician involved in the care and treatment of the patient, including documentation by consulting physicians, is appropriate for the basis of code assignment. If documentation from different physicians conflicts, seek clarification from the attending physician, as he or she is ultimately responsible for the final diagnosis.

Queries are also not necessary when a physician has documented a final diagnosis and clinical indicator—such as test results—do not appear to support this diagnosis. While coding professionals are expected to advocate complete and accurate physician documentation and to collaborate with physicians to realize this goal, they are not expected to challenge the physician's medical judgment in establishing the patient's diagnosis. However, because a discrepancy between clinical findings and a final diagnosis is a clinical issue, a facility may choose to establish a policy that the physician will be queried in these instances.

Documentation of Query Response

The physician's response to the query must be documented in the patient's medical record. Each facility must develop a policy regarding the specific process for incorporating this additional documentation in the medical record. For example, this policy might stipulate that the physician is required to add the additional information to the body of the medical record. As an alternative, a form, such as a medical record "progress note" form, might be attached to the query form and the attachment is then filed in the medical record. However, another alternative is to file the query form itself in the permanent medical record. Any documentation obtained post-discharge must be included in the discharge summary or identified as a late entry or addendum.

Any decision to file this form in the medical record should involve the advice of the facility's corporate compliance officer and legal counsel, due to potential compliance and legal risks related to incorporating the actual query form into the permanent medical record (such as its potential use as evidence of poor documentation in an audit, investigation, or malpractice suit, risks related to naming a nonclinician in the medical record, or quality of care concerns if the physician response on a query form is not clearly supported by the rest of the medical record documentation).

If the query form will serve as the only documentation of the physician's clarification, the use of "open-ended" questions (that require the physician to specifically document the additional information) are preferable to multiple choice questions or the use of questions requiring only a "yes" or "no" answer. The query form would need to be approved by the medical staff/medical records committee before implementation of a policy allowing this form to be maintained in the medical record. Also keep in mind that the Joint Commission hospital accreditation standards stipulate that only authorized individuals may make entries in medical records (IM.7.1.1). Therefore, the facility needs to consider modifying the medical staff bylaws to specify coding professionals as individuals authorized to make medical record entries prior to allowing query forms to become a permanent part of the medical record.

Auditing, Monitoring, and Corrective Action

Ideally, complete and accurate physician documentation should occur at the time care is rendered. The need for a query form results from incomplete, conflicting, or ambiguous documentation, which is an indication of poor documentation. Therefore, query form usage should be the exception rather than the norm. If physicians are being queried frequently, facility management or an appropriate medical staff committee should investigate the reasons why.

A periodic review of the query practice should include a determination of what percentage of the query forms are eliciting negative and positive responses from the physicians. A high negative response rate may be an indication that the coding staff are not using the query process judiciously and are being overzealous.

A high positive response rate may indicate that there are widespread poor documentation habits that need to be addressed. It may also indicate that the absence of certain reports (for example, discharge summary, operative report) at the time of coding is forcing the coding staff to query the physicians to obtain the information they need for proper coding.

If this is the case, the facility may wish to reconsider its policy regarding the availability of certain reports prior to coding. Waiting for these reports may make more sense in terms of turnaround time and productivity rather than finding it necessary to frequently query the physicians. The question of why final diagnoses are not available at the time of discharge may arise at the time of an audit, review by the peer review organization, or investigation.

The use of query forms should also be monitored for patterns, and any identified patterns should be used to educate physicians on improving their documentation at the point of care. If a pattern is identified, such as a particular physician or diagnosis, appropriate steps should be taken to correct the problem so the necessary documentation is present prior to coding in the future and the need to query this physician, or to query physicians regarding a particular diagnosis, is reduced. Corrective action might include targeted education for one physician or education for the entire medical staff on the proper documentation necessary for accurate code assignment.

Patterns of poor documentation that have not been addressed through education or other corrective action are signs of an ineffective compliance program. The Department of Health and Human Services Office of Inspector General has noted in its Compliance Program Guidance for Hospitals that "accurate coding depends upon the quality of completeness of the physician's documentation" and "active staff physician participation in educational programs focusing on coding and documentation should be emphasized by the hospital."[5]

The format of the queries should also be monitored on a regular basis to ensure that they are not inappropriately leading the physician to provide a particular response. Inappropriately written queries should be used to educate the coding staff on a properly written query. Patterns of inappropriately written queries should be referred to the corporate compliance officer.

Prepared by
Sue Prophet, RHIA, CCS

Acknowledgments
AHIMA Advocacy and Policy Task Force
AHIMA's Coding Practice Team
AHIMA Coding Policy and Strategy Committee
AHIMA Society for Clinical Coding
Dan Rode, MBA, FHFMA

Notes
1. Joint Commission on Accreditation of Healthcare Organizations. Comprehensive Accreditation Manual for Hospitals: The Official Handbook. Oakbrook Terrace, IL: Joint Commission, 2000.

2. Health Care Financing Administration, Department of Health and Human Services. "Conditions of Participation for Hospitals." Code of Federal Regulations, 2000. 42 CFR, Chapter IV, Part 482.

3. Official ICD-9-CM Guidelines for Coding and Reporting developed and approved by the American Hospital Association, American Health Information Management Association, Health Care Financing Administration, and the National Center for Health Statistics.

4. AHIMA is the professional organization responsible for issuing several credentials in health information management: Registered Health Information Administrator (RHIA), Registered Health Information Technician (RHIT), Certified Coding Specialist (CCS), and Certified Coding Specialist—Physician-based (CCS-P).

5. Office of Inspector General, Department of Health and Human Services. "Compliance Program Guidance for Hospitals." Washington, DC: Office of Inspector General, 1998.

References
AHIMA Code of Ethics, 1998.

AHIMA Standards of Ethical Coding, 1999.

AHIMA Coding Policy and Strategy Committee. "Practice Brief: Data Quality." *Journal of AHIMA* 67, no. 2 (1996).

Reprinted from: Prophet, Sue. "Developing a Physician Query Process (AHIMA Practice Brief)." *Journal of AHIMA* 72, no.9 (2001): 88I-M.

AHIMA Practice Brief: Developing a Coding Compliance Policy Document

Organizations using diagnosis and procedure codes for reporting healthcare services must have formal policies and corresponding procedures in place that provide instruction on the entire process—from the point of service to the billing statement or claim form. Coding compliance policies serve as a guide to performing coding and billing functions and provide documentation of the organization's intent to correctly report services. The policies should include facility-specific documentation requirements, payer regulations and policies, and contractual arrangements for coding consultants and outsourcing services. This information may be covered in payer/provider contracts or found in Medicare and Medicaid manuals and bulletins.

Following are selected tenets that address the process of code selection and reporting. These tenets may be referred to as coding protocols, a coding compliance program, organizational coding guidelines, or a similar name. These tenets are an important part of any organization's compliance plan and the key to preventing coding errors and resulting reimbursement problems. Examples are taken from both outpatient and inpatient coding processes for illustration purposes only. This document cannot serve as a complete coding compliance plan, but will be useful as a guide for creating a more comprehensive resource to meet individual organizational needs.

A coding compliance plan should include the following components:

- **A general policy statement about the commitment of the organization to correctly assign and report codes**

    Example: Memorial Medical Center is committed to establishing and maintaining clinical coding and insurance claims processing procedures to ensure that reported codes reflect actual services provided, through accurate information system entries.

- **The source of the official coding guidelines used to direct code selection**

    Example: ICD-9-CM code selection follows the Official Guidelines for Coding and Reporting, developed by the cooperating parties and documented in *Coding Clinic for ICD-9-CM,* published by the American Hospital Association.

    Example: CPT code selection follows the guidelines set forth in the CPT manual and in *CPT Assistant,* published by the American Medical Association.

- **The parties responsible for code assignment. The ultimate responsibility for code assignment lies with the physician (provider). However, policies and procedures may**

document instances where codes may be selected or modified by authorized individuals

Example: For inpatient records, medical record analyst I staff are responsible for analysis of records and assignment of the correct ICD-9-CM codes based on documentation by the attending physician.

Example: Emergency department evaluation and management levels for physician services will be selected by the physician and validated by outpatient record analysts using the HCFA/AMA documentation guidelines. When a variance occurs, the following steps are taken for resolution (The actual document should follow with procedure details).

- **The procedure to follow when the clinical information is not clear enough to assign the correct code**

Example: When the documentation used to assign codes is ambiguous or incomplete, the physician must be contacted to clarify the information and complete/amend the record, if necessary. (The actual document should follow with details of how the medical staff would like this to occur, e.g., by phone call, by note on the record, etc.). Standard protocols for adding documentation to a record must be followed, in accordance with the applicable laws and regulations.

- **Specify the policies and procedures that apply to specific locations and care settings. Official coding guidelines for inpatient reporting and outpatient/physician reporting are different. This means that if you are developing a facility-specific coding guideline for emergency department services, designate that the coding rules or guidelines only apply in this setting**

Example: When reporting an injection of a drug provided in the emergency department to a Medicare beneficiary, the appropriate CPT code for the administration of the injection is reported in addition to the evaluation and management service code and drug code. CPT codes are reported whether a physician provides the injection personally or a nurse is carrying out a physician's order. This instruction does not always apply for reporting of professional services in the clinics, because administration of medication is considered bundled with the corresponding evaluation and management service for Medicare patients.

Example: Diagnoses that are documented as "probable," "suspected," "questionable," "rule-out," or "working diagnosis" are not to have a code assigned as a confirmed diagnosis. Instead, the code for the condition established at the close of the encounter should be assigned, such as a symptom, sign, abnormal test result, or clinical finding. This guideline applies only to outpatient services.

- **Applicable reporting requirements required by specific agencies. The document should include where instructions on payer-specific requirements may be accessed**

Example: For patients with XYZ care plan, report code S0800 for patients having a LASIK procedure rather than an unlisted CPT code.

Example: For Medicare patients receiving a wound closure by tissue adhesive only, report HCPCS Level II code G0168 rather than a CPT code.

Many of these procedures will be put into software databases and would not be written as a specific policy. This is true with most billing software, whether for physician services or through the charge description master used by many hospitals.

- **Procedures for correction of inaccurate code assignments in the clinical database and to the agencies where the codes have been reported**

  Example: When an error in code assignment is discovered after bill release and the claim has already been submitted, this is the process required to update and correct the information system and facilitate claim amendment or correction (The actual document should follow with appropriate details).

- **Areas of risk that have been identified through audits or monitoring. Each organization should have a defined audit plan for code accuracy and consistency review and corrective actions should be outlined for problems that are identified**

  Example: A hospital might identify that acute respiratory failure is being assigned as the principal diagnosis with congestive heart failure as a secondary diagnosis. The specific reference to Coding Clinic could be listed with instructions about correct coding of these conditions and the process to be used to correct the deficiency.

- **Identification of essential coding resources available to and used by the coding professionals**

  Example: Updated ICD-9-CM, CPT, and HCPCS Level II code books are used by all coding professionals. Even if the hospital uses automated encoding software, at least one printed copy of the coding manuals should be available for reference.

  Example: Updated encoder software, including the appropriate version of the NCCI edits and DRG and APC grouper software, is available to the appropriate personnel.

  Example: Coding Clinic and CPT Assistant are available to all coding professionals.

- **A process for coding new procedures or unusual diagnoses**

  Example: When the coding professional encounters an unusual diagnosis, the coding supervisor or the attending physician is consulted. If, after research, a code cannot be identified, the documentation is submitted to the AHA for clarification.

- **A procedure to identify any optional codes gathered for statistical purposes by the facility and clarification of the appropriate use of E codes**

  Example: All ICD-9-CM procedure codes in the surgical range (ICD-9-CM Volume III codes 01.01-86.99) shall be reported for inpatients. In addition, codes reported from the non-surgical section include the following (Completed document should list the actual codes to be reported).

  Example: All appropriate E codes for adverse effects of drugs must be reported. In addition, this facility reports all E codes, including the place of injury for poisonings, all cases of abuse, and all accidents on the initial visit for both inpatient and outpatient services.

- **Appropriate methods for resolving coding or documentation disputes with physicians**

  Example: When the physician disagrees with official coding guidelines, the case is referred to the medical records committee following review by the designated physician liaison from that group.

- **A procedure for processing claim rejections**

  Example: All rejected claims pertaining to diagnosis and procedure codes should be returned to coding staff for review or correction. Any chargemaster issues should be forwarded to appropriate departmental staff for corrections. All clinical codes, including modifiers, must never be changed or added without review by coding staff with access to the appropriate documentation.

Example: If a claim is rejected due to the codes provided in the medical record abstract, the billing department notifies the supervisor of coding for a review rather than changing the code to a payable code and resubmitting the claim.

- **A statement clarifying that codes will not be assigned, modified, or excluded solely for the purpose of maximizing reimbursement. Clinical codes will not be changed or amended merely due to either physicians' or patients' request to have the service in question covered by insurance. If the initial code assignment did not reflect the actual services, codes may be revised based on supporting documentation. Disputes with either physicians or patients are handled only by the coding supervisor and are appropriately logged for review**

Example: A patient calls the business office saying that her insurance carrier did not pay for her mammogram. After investigating, the HIM coding staff discover that the coding was appropriate for a screening mammogram and that this is a non-covered service with the insurance provider. The code is not changed and the matter is referred back to the business office for explanation to the patient that she should contact her insurance provider with any dispute over coverage of service.

Example: Part of a payment is denied and after review, the supervisor discovers that a modifier should have been appended to the CPT code to denote a separately identifiable service. Modifier -25 is added to the code set and the corrected claim is resubmitted.

Example: A physician approaches the coding supervisor with a request to change the diagnosis codes for his patient because what she currently has is a pre-existing condition that is not covered by her current health plan. The coding supervisor must explain to the physician that falsification of insurance claims is illegal. If the physician insists, the physician liaison for the medical record committee is contacted and the matter is turned over to that committee for resolution if necessary.

- **The use of and reliance on encoders within the organization. Coding staff cannot rely solely on computerized encoders. Current coding manuals must be readily accessible and the staff must be educated appropriately to detect inappropriate logic or errors in encoding software. When errors in logic or code crosswalks are discovered, they are reported to the vendor immediately by the coding supervisor**

Example: During the coding process, an error is identified in the crosswalk between the ICD-9-CM Volume III code and the CPT code. This error is reported to the software vendor, with proper documentation and notification of all staff using the encoder to not rely on the encoder for code selection.

- **Medical records are analyzed and codes selected only with complete and appropriate documentation by the physician available. According to coding guidelines, codes are not assigned without physician documentation. If records are coded without the discharge summary or final diagnostic statements available, processes are in place for review after the summary is added to the record**

Example: When records are coded without a discharge summary, they are flagged in the computer system. When the summaries are added to the record, the record is returned to the coding professional for review of codes. If there are any inconsistencies, appropriate steps are taken for review of the changes.

Additional Elements

A coding compliance document should include a reference to the AHIMA Standards of Ethical Coding, which can be downloaded from AHIMA's Web site at www.ahima.org. Reference to the data quality assessment procedures must be included in a coding compliance plan to establish the mechanism for determining areas of risk. Reviews will identify the need for further education and increased monitoring for those areas where either coding variances or documentation deficiencies are identified.

Specific and detailed coding guidelines that cover the reporting of typical services provided by a facility or organization create tools for data consistency and reliability by ensuring that all coders interpret clinical documentation and apply coding principles in the same manner. The appropriate medical staff committee should give final approval of any coding guidelines that involve clinical criteria to assure appropriateness and physician consensus on the process.

The format is most useful when organized by patient or service type and easily referenced by using a table of contents. If the facility-specific guidelines are maintained electronically, they should be searchable by key terms. Placing the coding guidelines on a facility Intranet or internal computer network is a very efficient way to ensure their use and it also enables timely and efficient updating and distribution. Inclusion of references to or live links should be provided to supporting documents such as Uniform Hospital Discharge Data Sets or other regulatory requirements outlining reporting procedures or code assignments.

Prepared by

AHIMA's Coding Practice Team and reviewed by the Coding Policy and Strategy Committee and the Society for Clinical Coding Data Quality Committee

Reprinted from: AHIMA Coding Practice Team. "Developing a Coding Compliance Policy Document (AHIMA Practice Brief)." *Journal of AHIMA* 72, no.7 (2001): 88A-C.

American Health Information Management Association (AHIMA) Statement on Consistency of Healthcare Diagnostic and Procedural Coding

AHIMA's Position

AHIMA believes the collection of accurate and complete coded data is critical to healthcare delivery, research and analysis, reimbursement, and policymaking. The integrity of coded data and the ability to turn it into functional information requires that all users consistently apply the same official coding rules, conventions, guidelines, and definitions (the basis of coding standards). Use of uniform coding standards reduces administrative costs, enhances data quality and integrity, and improves decision-making—all leading to quality healthcare delivery and information.

For the United States to have and maintain quality data and information, coding standards must be required and promoted for uniform application and use, and not violated to meet parochial or short term requirements. In order for the nation to obtain, store, and utilize quality information, coding standards must be uniformly applied across sites of service and developed and maintained to meet the national and international needs of healthcare delivery, research, policy making, and the interpretation of healthcare data for the benefit of humankind. AHIMA's coding professionals are educated and certified to ethically apply and utilize national uniform coding standards to support these data quality, analysis, and maintenance functions.

Current Situation

Coded clinical data are used by healthcare providers, payers, researchers, government agencies, and others for:

- Measuring the quality, safety, and efficacy of care;
- Managing care and disease processes;
- Tracking public health and risks;
- Providing data to consumers regarding costs and outcomes of treatment options;

- Payment system design and processing of claims for reimbursement;

- Research, epidemiological studies, and clinical trials;

- Designing healthcare delivery systems and monitoring resource utilization;

- Identifying fraudulent practices; and

- Setting health policy.

The coding of clinical diagnostic and procedure data involves the translation of clinical information collected during healthcare encounters into diagnostic and procedural codes that accurately reflect the patients' medical conditions and services provided. A medical code set is an established system for encoding specific data elements pertaining to the provision of healthcare services, such as medical conditions, signs and symptoms, diagnostic, and therapeutic procedures, devices, and supplies. A code set includes the codes and code descriptions and, potentially, the rules, conventions, and guidelines for proper use of the codes.

Today, many coding practices are driven by health plan or payer reimbursement contracts or policies requiring providers to add, modify, or omit selected medical codes to reflect the plan or payer's coverages, policies or government regulations, contrary to standards for proper use of the code sets. Payers do not uniformly abide by such standards for proper application of the medical code sets. Code sets are not revised on the same date, and often payers require the continued use of deleted or invalid codes. Individual health plans, and even different contractors for the same plan (including Medicare and other government contractors), develop their own rules and definitions for the reporting of given codes. These variable requirements, which affect all the medical code sets currently required for reimbursement claims submission to third-party payers, undermine the integrity and comparability of healthcare data.

New uses of healthcare data are constantly evolving, further demanding that careful attention be paid to accurate and consistent application and reporting of coded data. Code sets must be sufficiently flexible to meet these changing needs, while maintaining stability and continuity over time to ensure data comparability. Those responsible for coding clinical data must be educated and trained to apply coding standards correctly and uniformly. The current situation, resulting in inconsistent coding practices, leads to potentially bad healthcare decisions today, and in the future.

Consistency of Healthcare Diagnostic and Procedure Coding Will Be Achieved When:

- All healthcare entities agree to:

  —Use only valid versions of the medical codes sets and coding standards, and

  —Refrain from establishing or accepting rules (for example, reimbursement rules), regulations, or contracts that force healthcare entities to violate coding standards.

- Certified coding professionals are utilized to assign and validate codes and assist in the development of policies that affect or depend on coding accuracy.

- Medical Code Set Maintenance Organizations:

  —Provide fully public processes for input to the update and maintenance of the code set standard;

  —Include representation by all groups of stakeholders in decisions regarding code set revisions; and

—Publish and implement code set revisions and standards on a scheduled basis for clarity of implementation requirements, due dates, and timely publishing of education materials by others outside the organization.

- Medical Code Sets are:

—Flexible to accommodate changes in healthcare that affect diagnoses, changes in medical and clinical practices, and so forth;

—Maintained to ensure stability and comparability of coded data over time;

—Maintained and updated on a timely basis to accommodate advances in medicine;

—Unique, so that users do not have to choose between or among different code sets;

—Capable of uniform use across different sites of service when the service is the same;

—Subject to a national central coordinating authority; and

—Serve to facilitate a national healthcare information in infrastructure.

Approved by the AHIMA Board of Directors, May 2002

The American Health Information Management Association is a dynamic organization of over 41,000 specially educated professionals—all working to ensure accurate and timely information within healthcare.

www.ahima.org

AHIMA Position Statement: Quality Healthcare Data and Information

The American Health Information Management Association (AHIMA) is a national association of more than 37,000 health record and health information management (HIM) professionals. AHIMA members work throughout the healthcare industry in settings ranging from physicians' offices and hospitals to ambulatory care facilities, long-term care facilities, and managed care organizations. HIM professionals ensure that patient health information is accurate, meets complex legal, licensure, and accreditation standards, and is accessible to healthcare providers, institutional administrators, and insurance companies. This information forms the basis of patient care, financial, and utilization decisions throughout the healthcare industry.

Issue: Quality Healthcare Data and Information

The American Health Information Management Association (AHIMA) advocates quality healthcare data and its transformation into meaningful healthcare information to improve the effectiveness and assess the quality of patient care. AHIMA believes that information is one of the most important resources of a healthcare organization.

In the course of healthcare delivery and management, various information systems deliver data that are used for administrative and patient care decisions. Information can be defined as organized data or knowledge that provides a basis for decision-making. AHIMA represents United States health information management professionals who have received specialized education and training and are certified as Registered Health Information Administrators (RHIA), Registered Health Information Technicians (RHIT), or Certified Coding Specialists (CCS). The members of AHIMA are specialists in collecting, analyzing, processing, integrating, storing, and securing healthcare data and information. This information serves as a means of communication between physicians and other healthcare professionals to document the course of the patient's illness and treatment during each current and subsequent episode of care. Members receive extensive training in the classification and coding of healthcare information for reimbursement, statistical, and research purposes.

Healthcare information and data serve important functions including:

- Evaluation of the adequacy and appropriateness of patient care

- Use in making decisions regarding healthcare policies, delivery systems, funding, expansion, education, and research

- Support for insurance and benefit claims

- Assistance in protecting the legal interests of the patients, healthcare professionals, and healthcare facilities

- Identification of disease incidence to control outbreaks and improve the public health

- Provision of case studies and epidemiological data for the education of health professionals

- Provision of data to expand the body of medical knowledge

To maintain data integrity and the quality of healthcare information, AHIMA members assume a leadership role in a variety of healthcare settings, including managed care, consulting, information systems development, and education, as well as through professional affiliations. AHIMA publishes educational material and is a resource to its members as well as others involved in the creation and utilization of health information. AHIMA interacts with other organizations in developing criteria and guidelines for documentation of patient care.

AHIMA believes the following are necessary components of healthcare data and information systems to ensure its quality, integrity, and reliability.

1. Collaboration by individuals providing healthcare with those processing and using health information

2. Provision of complete, accurate, and timely documentation of pertinent facts and observations about an individual's health, including past and present illnesses, tests, treatments, and outcomes

3. Assurance of the integrity of the data and protection of its unauthorized disclosure, whether it is a paper- or computer-based system

4. Establishment of clear, standard data collection guidelines for all levels of patient care in all sites of service, for example, inpatient, outpatient, emergency department, ambulatory clinics, medical practices, and home health

5. Support for the development and use of coding guidelines and adherence to the highest standards for accurate abstracting and coding of health information throughout the United States by all legitimate users, including healthcare organizations, third-party payers, and federal, state, and local governments

6. Respect for confidentiality of individually-identifiable health information

7. Commitment to ethical principles in the collection and dissemination of healthcare information

The quality of healthcare today and in the future is dependent on the quality of healthcare information.

AHIMA Practice Brief: Data Quality

Background

Complete and accurate diagnostic and procedural coded data are necessary for research, epidemiology, outcomes and statistical analyses, financial and strategic planning, reimbursement, evaluation of quality of care, and communication to support the patient's treatment. Upon the implementation of an inpatient prospective payment system, Medicare and several other payers required physicians to attest to the accuracy of the diagnoses and procedures being reported on inpatient claims prior to billing. The administrative burden of this requirement was recently deemed far greater than its success in preventing fraud and abuse, and thus the attestation requirement was eliminated. However, the loss of this requirement does not mean the need for accurate coded data has diminished. To the contrary, the quality of healthcare data is more critical than ever before. Adherence to approved coding principles that generate coded data of the highest quality remains important.

In this new era of clinical data management, health information professionals must continue to meet the challenges of maintaining an accurate and meaningful database reflective of patient mix and resource use. As long as diagnostic and procedural coding serves as the basis for payment methodologies, the ethics of clinical coders will be challenged. Assuring accuracy of coded data is a shared responsibility between health information management professionals and clinicians. The HIM professional continues to have the unique responsibility of assessing and coding clinical data. Within their organizations, health information management professionals translate clinical information into coded data and then evaluate, analyze, and maintain its accuracy, validity, and meaningfulness. Health information professionals are responsible for the achievement and maintenance of data of the highest quality.

Clinical Collaboration

The Joint Commission on Accreditation of Healthcare Organizations and the Medicare *Conditions of Participation* require final diagnoses and procedures to be recorded in the medical record and authenticated by the responsible practitioner. Physician documentation, in its entirety, is the cornerstone of accurate coding. Meaningful diagnostic and procedural coded data originate from the collaboration between clinicians with extensive clinical experience and coding professionals with comprehensive classification systems expertise.

Elimination of the attestation requirement does not mean the end to this collaboration, but rather a continued opportunity for dialogue and communication. Clinical documentation from which the coded data are derived continues to rely on information provided by healthcare practitioners. More than ever before, healthcare providers rely on coded clinical data for financial viability. Thus, the need for collaboration, cooperation, and communication between clinicians and coders continues to grow.

Clinical Database Evaluation

Ongoing evaluation of the clinical database may assure that ethical reporting of clinical information occurs. Regular evaluation of the quality of the database provides evidence that the clinical data remains consistent with standards of ethical coding practice.

Evaluation can be conducted by diagnosis-related group (DRG), pertinent clinical issues, high dollar cases, high volume DRGs, or particular diagnoses or procedures. The diagnosis and procedure codes should be reviewed to ensure the accuracy of coding, appropriate sequencing, and clinical pertinence. Reporting review results to administration and the medical staff increases their awareness of coded data quality issues within the facility.

Recommendations

The coding professional should:

- Thoroughly review the entire health record as part of the coding process in order to assign and report the most appropriate codes

- Adhere to all official coding guidelines as approved by the Cooperating Parties?

- Observe sequencing rules identified by the Cooperating Parties?

- Select the principal diagnosis and procedure according to UHDDS definitions?

- Assign and report codes, without physician consultation, to diagnoses and procedures not stated in the physician's final diagnosis only if these diagnoses and procedures are specifically documented by the physician in the body of the medical record and this documentation is clear and consistent

- Utilize medical record documentation to provide coding specificity without obtaining physician concurrence (such as utilizing the radiology report to identify the fracture site)

- Maintain a positive working relationship with physicians through ongoing communication and open dialogue

The coding professional should not:

- Add diagnosis codes solely based on test results

- Misrepresent the patient's clinical picture through incorrect coding or add diagnoses/ procedures unsupported by the documentation in order to maximize reimbursement or meet insurance policy coverage requirements

- Report diagnoses and procedures that the physician has specifically indicated he/she does not support

As the need for coded data of the highest quality continues to grow, HIM professionals need to build and develop their role as clinical data managers. In order to achieve this end, coder education in the areas of anatomy and physiology, medical terminology, disease pathology, pharmacology, and laboratory studies, as well as classification and reimbursement systems, should be encouraged. Dialogue between health information professionals and clinicians should also be encouraged, as it improves coder clinical competency and educates the clinician on documentation practice issues.

Additional Recommendations in the Absence of Physician Attestation

The coding professional should:

- Assess physician documentation to assure that it supports the diagnosis and procedure codes selected

- Consult the physician for clarification when conflicting or ambiguous documentation is present; ask the physician to add information to the record before assigning a code that is not supported by documentation

- Provide the physician the opportunity to review reported diagnoses and procedures on pre-or post-bill submission, via mechanisms such as:

  —Providing a copy (via mail, fax, or electronic transmission) of the sequenced codes and their narrative descriptions

  —Placing the diagnostic and procedural listing within the record and bringing it to the physician's attention

- Revise the codes if the physician disagrees with code selection

- Offer coding and classification system education to any and all clinicians (for example, provide pertinent official coding guidelines)

- Develop institutional coding policies in the absence of official guidelines

Notes

1. American Hospital Association; American Health Information Management Association; Health Care Financing Administration; National Center for Health Statistics

2. Uniform Data Discharge Set

Prepared by: Coding Policy and Strategy Committee

Reviewed by: Society for Clinical Coding

AHIMA Resolution:
Advocating for Quality Documentation and Adherence to Official Coding Guidelines

Background Information

In August 1996, the Health Insurance Portability and Accountability Act (HIPAA) [Public Law 104-191] established the infrastructure and funding for federal fraud and abuse efforts. This legislation authorizes the appropriation of $104 million in 1997, with increases in 15 percent increments until 2003, to defray the costs of the Department of Health and Human Services (HHS) Office of Inspector General's (OIG's) and the Federal Bureau of Investigation's enforcement activities. Section 201(b) establishes the Health Care Fraud and Abuse Control Account within the Medicare Trust Fund. Under the legislation, this account will receive proceeds from: (1) criminal fines from "federal health care offenses;" (2) civil money penalties from cases involving Medicare and Medicaid or the peer review provisions; (3) forfeitures of property arising from federal healthcare offenses; and (4) penalties and damages obtained from health-related False Claims Act actions.

Section 201 of HIPAA also creates the Fraud and Abuse Control Program through which Congress grants the OIG and the U.S. Attorney General joint authority to coordinate federal, state, and local law enforcement programs to control all healthcare fraud and abuse. Section 203 mandates the creation of a program to encourage individuals to report suspected fraud and abuse violations. The Secretary of HHS is directed to establish a program for encouraging individuals to report persons who are, or have been, engaged in any activity that constitutes fraud and abuse against Medicare.

Sections 241 through 250 of HIPAA revise the federal criminal law to provide for a federal healthcare offense relating to a healthcare benefit program. The definition of healthcare benefit program includes federal healthcare programs and "any public or private plan or contract, affecting commerce, under which any medical benefit, item, or service is provided to any individual, and includes any individual or entity who is providing a medical benefit, item, or service for which payment may be made under the plan or contract." HIPAA establishes new criminal provisions covering a wide range of activities: healthcare fraud, theft, or embezzlement in connection with healthcare; false statements relating to healthcare matters; obstruction of criminal investigations of healthcare offenses; and laundering of monetary instruments related to a federal healthcare offense.

Section 231 of HIPAA increases the intent standard that the government must meet for civil monetary penalties. To establish liability, the government must demonstrate that the defendant "knowingly" submitted false claims. Knowingly is defined so that one may be liable if a false claim or statement is made: (1) with actual knowledge that it is false; (2) in deliberate ignorance of the truth or falsity of the information; or (3) in reckless disregard of the truth or falsity of the information.

In the regulatory arena, OIG expects to complete more than 100 reviews of various healthcare providers, including hospitals, physicians, home health care agencies, clinical labs, and managed care plans to detect whether they are correctly billing the Medicare and Medicaid program for services. The healthcare fraud and abuse initiative, Operation Restore Trust, will add twelve mores states to the five already targeted by the two-year-old program. The program focuses on home health providers, nursing homes, and durable medical equipment suppliers.

During the past several months, the federal government has instituted the second half of its enforcement activities concerning billing under Medicare Part B for physician services performed at teaching hospitals. In 1996, HCFA adopted a variety of standards that teaching hospitals must now meet to bill for physician services under Medicare Part B. More recently, OIG announced that it will conduct audits nationwide to evaluate compliance of teaching hospitals in past years with regulatory requirements.

The healthcare field is highly regulated by a complex statutory and regulatory scheme. HIM professionals, at the crossroads of healthcare and information management, are profoundly impacted by the interpretation and implementation of government policy for reimbursement of institutional and provider claims. HIM professionals are uniquely qualified to provide leadership in healthcare organizations to ensure that the documentation in the health record is accurate and appropriate to support the diagnoses and procedures selected for reimbursement.

Resolution

Topic: Advocating for Quality Documentation and Adherence to Official Coding Guidelines

Intent: Promote the quality of documentation to support the appropriate use of codes for institutional and provider reimbursement

Addressed to: All HIM professionals and AHIMA's strategic partners

Approved by: 1997 House of Delegates

Date: October 19, 1997

Whereas, detection of healthcare fraud and abuse is a major activity at the federal, state, and local areas of government;

Whereas, ever-changing guidelines for reimbursement impact the ability of healthcare organizations to submit appropriate claims;

Whereas, insurers and payers do not uniformly adhere to official coding guidelines;

Whereas, AHIMA and its component organizations encourage healthcare providers, organizations, insurers, and other appropriate parties to adhere to official coding guidelines in submitting institutional and provider claims for reimbursement;

Whereas, AHIMA members promote accurate and ethical coding; therefore, be it

Resolved, That AHIMA members promote accurate and complete documentation that reflects the level of services provided to the patient and ensure that the HIM profession continues to play a pivotal role in addressing fraud and abuse; and

Resolved, That AHIMA and its component organizations advocate that the federal government and insurers adopt nationwide official coding standards and guidelines used in the development and interpretation of policy for institutional reimbursement and provider claims.

Appendix E
Ethics

AHIMA Code of Ethics

AHIMA Standards of Ethical Coding

AHIMA Code of Ethics

Preamble

This Code of Ethics sets forth ethical principles for the health information management profession. Members of this profession are responsible for maintaining and promoting ethical practices. This Code of Ethics, adopted by the American Health Information Management Association, shall be binding on health information management professionals who are members of the Association and all individuals who hold an AHIMA credential.

  I.   Health information management professionals respect the rights and dignity of all individuals.

  II.   Health information management professionals comply with all laws, regulations, and standards governing the practice of health information management.

  III.   Health Information management professionals strive for professional excellence through self-assessment and continuing education.

  IV.   Health information management professionals truthfully and accurately represent their professional credentials, education, and experience.

  V.   Health information management professionals adhere to the vision, mission, and values of the Association.

  VI.   Health information management professionals promote and protect the confidentiality and security of health records and health information.

  VII.   Health information management professionals strive to provide accurate and timely information.

  VIII. Health information management professionals promote high standards for health information management practice, education, and research

  IX.   Health information management professionals act with integrity and avoid conflicts of interest in the performance of their professional and AHIMA responsibilities.

Revised October 1998.

AHIMA Standards of Ethical Coding

In this era of payment based on diagnostic and procedural coding, the professional ethics of health information coding professionals continue to be challenged. A conscientious goal for coding and maintaining a quality database is accurate clinical and statistical data. The following standards of ethical coding, developed by the AHIMA Coding Policy and Strategy Committee and approved by the AHIMA Board of Directors, are offered to guide coding professionals in this process.

1. Coding professionals are expected to support the importance of accurate, complete, and consistent coding practices for the production of quality healthcare data.

2. Coding professionals in all healthcare settings should adhere to the ICD-9-CM *(International Classification of Diseases, Ninth Revision, Clinical Modification)* coding conventions, official coding guidelines approved by the Cooperating Parties*, the CPT *(Current Procedural Terminology)* rules established by the American Medical Association, and any other official coding rules and guidelines established for use with mandated standard code sets. Selection and sequencing of diagnoses and procedures must meet the definitions of required data sets for applicable healthcare settings.

3. Coding professionals should use their skills, their knowledge of the currently mandated coding and classification systems, and official resources to select the appropriate diagnostic and procedural codes.

4. Coding professionals should only assign and report codes that are clearly and consistently supported by physician documentation in the health record.

5. Coding professionals should consult physicians for clarification and additional documentation prior to code assignment when there is conflicting or ambiguous data in the health record.

*The Cooperating Parties are the American Health Information Management Association, American Hospital Association, Centers for Medicare and Medicaid Services, and National Center for Health Statistics.

6. Coding professionals should not change codes or the narratives of codes on the billing abstract so that the meanings are misrepresented. Diagnoses or procedures should not be inappropriately included or excluded because the payment or insurance policy coverage requirements will be affected. When individual payer policies conflict with official coding rules and guidelines, these policies should be obtained in writing whenever possible. Reasonable efforts should be made to educate the payer on proper coding practices in order to influence a change in the payer's policy.

7. Coding professionals, as members of the healthcare team, should assist and educate physicians and other clinicians by advocating proper documentation practices, further specificity, resequencing or inclusion of diagnoses or procedures when needed to more accurately reflect the acuity, severity and the occurrence of events.

8. Coding professionals should participate in the development of institutional coding policies and should ensure that coding policies complement, not conflict with, official coding rules and guidelines.

9. Coding professionals should maintain and continually enhance their coding skills, as they have a professional responsibility to stay abreast of changes in codes, coding guidelines, and regulations.

10. Coding professionals should strive for the optimal payment to which the facility is legally entitled, remembering that it is unethical and illegal to maximize payment by means that contradict regulatory guidelines.

Revised December 1999.

Appendix F
Suggested Resources

The following are not all-inclusive lists of resources. Numerous vendors, as well as additional organizations, offer compliance-related, benchmarking, and profiling products and services. Use of an Internet search engine is an effective means of finding information on available products and services. Many companies also advertise in healthcare and professional trade publications. At least thirty-seven states have been mandated to collect hospital-level data. Depending on the state, this data may or may not be available to the public. State hospital associations can provide information concerning the availability of comparative data.

Publication of the names of specific vendors does not constitute an endorsement by AHIMA of any particular product or service.

Organizations

American Association of Health Plans
1129 Twentieth St., NW, Suite 600
Washington, DC 20036-3421
(202) 778-3269
Web site: www.aahp.org

American Health Information Management
Association
233 N. Michigan Ave., Suite 2150
Chicago, IL 60601-5800
(312) 233-1100
Web site: www.ahima.org

American Health Lawyers Association
1120 Connecticut Ave., SW, Suite 950
Washington, DC 20036-3902
(202) 833-1100
Web site: www.healthlawyers.org

American Hospital Association
One North Franklin
Chicago, IL 60606
(312) 422-3000
Web site: www.aha.org

American Medical Association
515 N. State St.
Chicago, IL 60610
(312) 464-5000
Web site: www.ama-assn.org

American Medical Group Association
1422 Duke St.
Alexandria, VA 22314
(703) 838-0033
Web site: www.amga.org

Association of American Medical Colleges
2450 N. Street, NW
Washington, DC 20037-1126
(202) 828-0400
Web site: www.aamc.org

Association of Healthcare Internal Auditors
900 Fox Valley Drive, Suite 204
Longwood, FL 32779-2554
(407) 786-8200
Web site: www.ahia.org

BlueCross/BlueShield Association
676 N. St. Clair Street
Chicago, IL 60611
(312) 440-6000
Web site: www.bluecares.com

Coalition Against Insurance Fraud
1012 14th St., NW, Suite 200
Washington, DC 20005
(202) 393-7330
Web site: www.insurancefraud.org

Healthcare Billing and Management
Association
1550 S. Coast Hwy, Suite 201
Laguna Beach, CA 92651
(877) 640-HBMA
Web site: www.hbma.com

Health Care Compliance Association
1211 Locust St.
Philadelphia, PA 19107
(888) 580-8373
Web site: www.hcca-info.org

Healthcare Financial Management Association
2 Westbrook Corporate Center, Suite 700
Westchester, IL 60154
(708) 531-9600
Web site: www.hfma.org

Health Insurance Association of America
555 13th St., NW
Washington, DC 20004
(202) 824-1600
Web site: www.hiaa.org

Medical Group Management Association
104 Inverness Terrace East
Englewood, CO 80112-5306
(888) 608-5601
Web site: www.mgma.com

National Health Care Anti-Fraud Association
1255 23rd St., NW
Washington, DC 20037
(202) 659-5955
Web site: www.nhcaa.org

Professional Association of Health Care
Office Managers
461 East Ten Mile Rd.
Pensacola, FL 32534-9712
(800) 451-9311
Web site: www.pahcom.com

Taxpayers against Fraud
The False Claims Act Legal Center
1220 19th St., NW, Suite 501
Washington, DC 20036
(202) 296-4826
Web site: www.taf.org

The American Compliance Institute
13728 Smoketown Rd., PMB #1479
Woodbridge, VA 22192
(800) 660-9551
Web site: www.compliance.com

Other Resources

Central Office on ICD-9-CM
American Hospital Association
One North Franklin
Chicago, IL 60606
(312) 422-3366
Web site: www.icd-9-cm.org

National Correct Coding Initiative
United States Department of Commerce
National Technical Information Service
5285 Port Royal Rd.
Springfield, VA 22161
(800) 363-2068
Web site: www.ntis.gov

To subscribe to the American Medical
Association's CPT Information Services for
answers to CPT coding questions:
(800) 621-8335

Government Web Sites

Centers for Medicare and Medicaid Services:
www.hcfa.gov

Medicare Manuals:
www.hcfa.gov/pubforms/progman.htm

National Coverage Determinations:
www.cms.hhs.gov/coverage/8b3.asp

Home Health PPS:
www.hcfa.gov/medicare/hhmain.htm

Rehabilitation PPS:
www.hcfa.gov/medicare/irfpps.htm

HHS Office of Inspector General:
http://www.hhs.gov/oig

Additional Internet Resources

Health Care Integrity and Protection Data Bank and National Practitioner Data Bank:
www.npdb-hipdb.com

HHS Office of Inspector General's RATSTATS Program: www.hhs.gov/organization/OAS/ratstat.pdf

Medicare Hospital Manual ordering information: www.hcfa.gov/pubforms/p2192ch2.htm

HIPAA rules and other resources: http://aspe.os.dhhs.gov/admnsimp/

Medicare local medical review policies: www.lmrp.net

Listservs

Fraud-l: To subscribe, go to http://www.compliancealert.net and click on "Join the Fraud and Abuse Listserv."

American Health Lawyers Association Compliance listserv: send the message "subscribe compliance" (without quotes) in the body of an e-mail message to this e-mail address: Commands@HealthLawyers.org

Sources of Comparative Data

Comparative data are necessary to establish internal coding data monitors. Data may be obtained from a variety of sources, usually for a charge. Many private companies offer access to giant databases, often in a user-friendly electronic format. Many states, through state data organizations or hospital associations, release claims data for all payers. Peer review organizations often provide comparative data reports. The most notable comparative data is Medicare MedPar data, which can be obtained from the CMS at:

Centers for Medicare and Medicaid Services
Public Use Files
Accounting Division
P.O. Box 7520
Baltimore, MD 21207-0520
(410) 786-3691

CMS also provides some public use files free of charge. These can be accessed from CMS's home page at www.hcfa.gov/stats/stats.htm. CMS's interim resource-based practice expense data files, "CPT Procedure Code Utilization by Specialty," can be accessed at: http://www.hcfa.gov/stats/resource.htm

Other sources of health data include:

*   American Hospital Directory (www.ahd.com)
    Analysis of facility-specific financial and DRG data

*   Data Advantage (www.data-advantage.com)
    Comparative healthcare information products

*   Solucient (www.solucient.com)
    (800) 366-PLAN
    Hospital benchmarking and profiling products

- The Center for Healthcare Industry Performance Studies
  (800) 859-2447
  Hospital benchmarking and profiling products

- The MEDSTAT Group
  (800) 650-1550
  Hospital benchmarking and profiling products

- Iameter Inc.
  (415) 349-9100
  Hospital benchmarking and profiling products

- National Center for Health Statistics (www.cdc.gov/nchs)
  Data warehouse

- National Health Information Resource Center (www.nhirc.org)
  Links to sixty health data sites

- QuadraMed Corporation
  (800) 473-7633
  Hospital benchmarking

In addition, the National Association of Health Data Organizations (www.nahdo.org) has published two books with information on health data sources: *State Health Data Resource Manual: Hospital Discharge Data Systems* and *A Guide to State-level Ambulatory Care Data Collection Activities.*

Appendix G
Medicare Provider Analysis and Review (MEDPAR) Data: Fiscal Year 2000

The following information for short-stay hospitals was compiled by the Bureau of Data Management and Strategy of the Centers for Medicare and Medicaid Services (CMS). Additional competitive data for 1990 through 1998 is available from CMS's Web site (www.hcfa.gov).

CMS 100% MEDPAR Inpatient Hospital Fiscal Year 2000 (June 2001 Update)

			Short Stay Inpatient by State			
State	Total Charges	Covered Charges	Medicare Reimbursement	Total Days	Number of Discharges	Average Total Days
Alabama	$4,321,665,194	$4,299,086,294	$1,504,515,008	1,512,780	274,518	5.5
Alaska	$206,293,809	$201,034,703	$110,638,774	70,006	11,684	6.0
Arizona	$2,540,433,308	$2,524,660,375	$874,063,537	665,543	135,143	4.9
Arkansas	$2,106,019,614	$2,090,434,054	$850,455,354	974,921	164,310	5.9
California	$20,627,938,233	$20,381,913,109	$6,639,146,137	4,426,018	740,564	6.0
Colorado	$1,670,713,556	$1,661,238,915	$685,000,973	498,189	101,486	4.9
Connecticut	$1,969,169,497	$1,951,453,679	$1,084,569,154	766,645	124,951	6.1
Delaware	$430,201,176	$426,997,571	$240,209,009	223,231	34,049	6.6
Washington D.C.	$962,726,796	$950,085,491	$447,411,614	291,192	39,112	7.4
Florida	$15,144,119,086	$15,017,099,271	$5,000,041,590	4,454,500	765,130	5.8
Georgia	$4,681,482,651	$4,645,141,460	$2,094,629,003	1,889,191	324,286	5.8
Hawaii	$602,797,303	$580,603,825	$219,715,456	215,814	26,146	8.3
Idaho	$476,373,503	$475,542,087	$239,709,689	196,963	44,027	4.5
Ilinois	$9,469,909,499	$9,363,552,527	$3,616,977,573	3,180,422	556,122	5.7
Indiana	$3,781,716,641	$3,758,604,742	$1,813,098,652	1,690,912	297,851	5.7
Iowa	$1,778,479,286	$1,769,882,659	$856,800,142	851,467	159,451	5.3
Kansas	$1,791,563,460	$1,779,310,048	$737,921,267	706,644	128,024	5.5
Kentucky	$3,060,306,851	$3,035,339,735	$1,345,778,302	1,374,967	243,886	5.6
Louisiana	$3,790,841,733	$3,744,586,818	$1,477,245,488	1,410,023	237,154	5.9
Maine	$865,001,558	$860,638,094	$410,638,403	379,690	69,030	5.5
Maryland	$1,935,104,942	$1,918,398,755	$1,662,618,297	1,215,152	208,038	5.8
Massachusetts	$3,652,137,345	$3,604,450,888	$2,106,850,372	1,517,298	263,152	5.8
Michigan	$6,782,936,939	$6,736,242,102	$3,369,079,328	2,797,892	452,367	6.2
Minnesota	$2,906,265,785	$2,878,854,096	$1,362,036,462	1,019,244	200,918	5.1
Mississippi	$2,306,808,003	$2,292,388,851	$907,772,858	1,164,116	183,952	6.3
Missouri	$4,788,323,375	$4,755,838,409	$1,979,965,012	1,742,359	300,576	5.8
Montana	$467,760,899	$467,383,356	$250,516,874	212,607	44,208	4.8
Nebraska	$1,197,097,579	$1,191,012,907	$533,993,419	407,589	76,960	5.3
Nevada	$1,264,456,996	$1,252,790,693	$367,932,435	300,727	49,613	6.1
New Hampshire	$621,869,332	$617,435,188	$329,117,371	258,574	45,712	5.7
New Jersey	$10,371,668,832	$10,211,947,120	$3,135,704,396	2,780,652	372,063	7.5
New Mexico	$651,184,981	$646,656,219	$287,595,079	261,010	51,085	5.1
New York	$12,950,085,915	$12,669,581,819	$7,217,679,451	6,252,660	750,793	8.3
North Carolina	$5,262,452,918	$5,221,876,812	$2,541,086,427	2,470,485	406,700	6.1
North Dakota	$440,360,417	$438,851,722	$231,535,018	206,301	39,672	5.2
Ohio	$6,972,892,917	$6,931,461,699	$3,484,991,700	3,004,872	536,335	5.6
Oklahoma	$2,369,576,897	$2,356,653,510	$1,002,873,473	1,030,817	176,021	5.9
Oregon	$1,124,711,685	$1,119,707,696	$617,434,103	422,460	91,806	4.6
Pennsylvania	$11,659,760,413	$11,566,965,176	$4,554,487,716	3,926,041	634,802	6.2
Puerto Rico	$885,902,472	$873,921,388	$368,724,701	937,874	137,315	6.8
Rhode Island	$549,060,638	$543,604,872	$284,341,186	238,398	38,489	6.2

Short Stay Inpatient by State

State	Total Charges	Covered Charges	Medicare Reimbursement	Total Days	Number of Discharges	Average Total Days
South Carolina	$3,261,450,227	$3,237,802,674	$1,294,742,088	1,275,145	204,038	6.2
South Dakota	$510,161,481	$509,135,175	$248,187,138	239,294	45,239	5.3
Tennessee	$4,810,164,577	$4,774,596,745	$2,047,716,329	1,975,703	327,423	6.0
Texas	$13,074,798,089	$12,950,638,946	$4,994,878,168	4,395,093	742,628	5.9
Utah	$721,921,650	$721,048,611	$360,314,027	260,023	53,003	4.9
Vermont	$280,668,272	$275,947,475	$169,720,065	146,504	24,014	6.1
Virgin Islands	$18,271,376	$17,854,779	$10,947,813	18,408	1,552	11.9
Virginia	$4,299,348,566	$4,268,032,351	$1,827,517,447	1,805,295	295,790	6.1
Washington	$2,013,535,135	$1,996,187,610	$1,161,544,744	754,230	153,660	4.9
West Virginia	$1,386,572,524	$1,379,071,421	$726,643,331	777,513	134,585	5.8
Wisconsin	$3,066,336,835	$3,047,909,673	$1,485,552,758	1,288,304	238,572	5.4
Wyoming	$216,264,211	$216,139,410	$109,719,516	92,962	18,764	5.0
Unknown	$12,787,079	$12,712,648	$6,383,203	12,583	1,936	6.5
TOTAL	$193,110,452,056	$191,220,306,253	$81,288,767,430	70,987,303	11,778,705	6.0

Short Stay Inpatient by National DRG

DRG	Total Charges	Covered Charges	Medicare Reimbursement	Total Days	Number of Discharges	Average Total Days
001	$1,314,283,095	$1,303,743,551	$603,236,270	309,517	34,350	9.0
002	$271,492,465	$269,190,826	$119,184,394	68,960	6,906	10.0
003						
004	$173,608,099	$172,000,643	$77,526,681	44,266	6,180	7.2
005	$1,463,833,451	$1,456,861,297	$608,172,939	297,860	94,068	3.2
006	$3,167,677	$3,149,746	$1,275,459	1,084	366	3.0
007	$393,860,541	$389,535,058	$173,259,148	130,853	13,189	9.9
008	$68,044,719	$67,566,844	$24,882,369	11,129	3,758	3.0
009	$28,931,706	$28,604,294	$11,308,790	12,989	1,768	7.3
010	$262,918,089	$260,992,050	$107,069,137	119,863	18,155	6.6
011	$33,276,799	$32,930,303	$12,630,478	13,769	3,237	4.3
012	$791,249,903	$780,908,497	$350,675,696	540,447	66,937	8.1
013	$66,542,633	$65,212,475	$24,010,322	35,697	6,664	5.4
014	$4,337,033,680	$4,308,620,914	$1,693,462,372	1,926,878	324,325	5.9
015	$1,213,087,579	$1,205,824,257	$431,908,832	522,098	146,750	3.6
016	$151,113,929	$149,341,959	$58,582,570	70,117	11,430	6.1
017	$27,804,987	$27,632,194	$9,168,556	12,267	3,593	3.4
018	$298,000,546	$294,006,614	$115,013,512	147,129	26,897	5.5
019	$68,173,102	$67,431,834	$23,542,133	31,588	8,462	3.7
020	$177,065,706	$175,043,318	$79,269,385	59,363	5,778	10.3
021	$22,007,393	$21,884,178	$9,965,628	8,701	1,336	6.5
022	$28,986,766	$28,760,056	$10,633,811	12,515	2,573	4.9
023	$94,426,630	$93,841,626	$35,899,767	44,318	10,088	4.4
024	$628,160,203	$620,101,656	$248,697,820	268,224	53,657	5.0

		Short Stay Inpatient by National DRG				
DRG	Total Charges	Covered Charges	Medicare Reimbursement	Total Days	Number of Discharges	Average Total Days
025	$185,354,106	$183,315,147	$64,266,510	83,350	25,748	3.2
026	$347,696	$346,183	$132,482	120	40	3.0
027	$58,375,325	$57,572,800	$25,178,169	18,313	3,552	5.2
028	$183,295,999	$181,374,547	$73,300,375	73,449	11,646	6.3
029	$40,275,224	$39,601,902	$13,673,788	17,681	4,637	3.8
030						
031	$38,612,406	$37,755,470	$12,777,153	16,296	3,633	4.5
032	$11,331,380	$11,122,233	$3,216,624	4,585	1,786	2.6
033						
034	$256,779,809	$253,954,250	$107,417,493	114,507	21,482	5.3
035	$48,151,116	$47,418,408	$17,225,486	23,919	6,263	3.8
036	$27,105,273	$26,888,522	$9,758,722	4,773	3,232	1.5
037	$21,138,529	$20,958,132	$8,188,798	5,954	1,480	4.0
038	$616,598	$590,159	$204,871	272	103	2.6
039	$7,191,362	$7,042,470	$2,450,001	1,845	934	2.0
040	$17,835,558	$17,703,008	$6,701,867	5,367	1,569	3.4
041	$0	$0	$0	0	0	0.0
042	$18,031,360	$17,862,648	$6,371,911	5,128	2,243	2.3
043	$488,983	$481,960	$155,498	276	86	3.2
044	$10,164,542	$10,001,326	$3,882,367	6,226	1,253	5.0
045	$19,789,284	$19,671,500	$7,106,782	7,849	2,473	3.2
046	$28,968,388	$28,642,543	$10,682,223	14,695	3,144	4.7
047	$7,990,500	$7,931,420	$2,481,933	4,403	1,322	3.3
048	$0	$0	$0	0	0	0.0
049	$54,065,692	$53,772,330	$23,809,849	11,447	2,355	4.9
050	$25,831,091	$25,714,515	$9,373,593	5,001	2,558	2.0
051	$2,012,873	$2,010,364	$778,884	553	206	2.7
052	$2,164,946	$2,155,707	$771,782	438	228	1.9
053	$37,839,019	$37,526,409	$15,326,319	9,152	2,546	3.6
054						
055	$16,967,306	$16,773,521	$6,580,209	4,232	1,557	2.7
056	$5,569,669	$5,449,365	$2,060,647	1,434	522	2.7
057	$10,080,219	$10,030,437	$4,196,146	2,902	717	4.0
058	$0	$0	$0	0	0	0.0
059	$1,097,913	$1,079,444	$356,776	300	108	2.8
060						
061	$3,676,196	$3,635,428	$1,572,907	1,220	234	5.2
062						
063	$52,299,245	$51,432,292	$20,750,091	13,332	3,017	4.4
064	$45,356,789	$44,820,991	$20,928,743	19,723	3,160	6.2
065	$213,395,070	$212,058,221	$67,493,864	99,165	34,827	2.8
066	$44,922,652	$44,630,835	$15,821,983	22,307	7,063	3.2

		Short Stay Inpatient by National DRG				
DRG	Total Charges	Covered Charges	Medicare Reimbursement	Total Days	Number of Discharges	Average Total Days
067	$4,364,811	$4,359,585	$1,702,484	1,802	505	3.6
068	$124,284,617	$123,385,387	$44,213,026	69,660	16,891	4.1
069	$30,152,154	$29,901,708	$9,868,238	17,955	5,480	3.3
070	$159,891	$151,721	$44,535	71	25	2.8
071	$612,932	$575,039	$176,334	312	82	3.8
072	$7,290,345	$7,206,914	$2,467,738	3,194	898	3.6
073	$61,329,543	$60,647,078	$23,120,532	29,865	6,747	4.4
074	$0	$0	$0	0	0	0.0
075	$1,446,127,196	$1,434,997,042	$657,005,763	397,663	40,343	9.9
076	$1,303,012,157	$1,278,486,355	$576,060,107	449,141	39,717	11.3
077	$32,423,477	$32,166,297	$13,158,438	11,307	2,332	4.8
078	$477,007,372	$473,758,178	$201,175,089	220,556	32,502	6.8
079	$3,153,694,276	$3,120,337,113	$1,323,306,929	1,458,524	171,606	8.5
080	$82,900,078	$82,415,537	$31,837,060	47,655	8,543	5.6
081						
082	$983,031,678	$975,304,365	$409,088,591	438,566	63,193	6.9
083	$72,208,473	$71,114,963	$25,508,187	37,166	6,686	5.6
084	$10,050,765	$9,818,980	$2,661,354	5,269	1,571	3.4
085	$284,800,992	$282,858,391	$120,526,693	132,093	20,899	6.3
086	$16,333,170	$15,963,705	$6,142,858	7,787	2,123	3.7
087	$897,499,142	$889,578,719	$362,189,481	383,176	60,731	6.3
088	$3,944,728,516	$3,911,065,253	$1,548,616,158	2,039,549	397,090	5.1
089	$6,147,583,873	$6,103,185,053	$2,472,562,495	3,164,183	531,770	6.0
090	$370,443,285	$367,849,330	$134,213,095	220,340	53,339	4.1
091	$640,644	$620,312	$202,095	265	60	4.4
092	$190,544,387	$188,864,388	$75,073,519	89,144	14,044	6.3
093	$13,358,458	$13,252,013	$5,098,739	6,570	1,614	4.1
094	$157,495,281	$156,191,829	$64,001,630	77,397	12,260	6.3
095	$10,780,676	$10,608,610	$3,650,057	6,049	1,631	3.7
096	$517,930,178	$513,416,094	$195,614,370	290,822	62,801	4.6
097	$196,777,484	$194,987,601	$68,697,780	115,077	31,569	3.6
098	$220,891	$220,891	$101,947	88	21	4.2
099	$152,267,845	$151,168,703	$54,400,434	62,196	19,363	3.2
100	$45,678,571	$45,300,892	$14,754,421	16,716	7,637	2.2
101	$199,091,518	$196,717,158	$75,594,791	90,008	20,417	4.4
102	$32,143,618	$31,398,540	$10,227,489	13,923	5,225	2.7
103	$143,809,679	$131,678,196	$66,841,076	23,729	526	45.1
104	$3,132,121,882	$3,109,686,912	$1,458,216,660	418,010	36,953	11.3
105	$2,010,786,582	$1,998,528,791	$925,968,256	277,592	29,935	9.3
106	$291,593,721	$289,784,988	$128,098,469	39,562	3,438	11.5
107	$5,445,439,643	$5,419,396,265	$2,405,992,714	922,749	88,980	10.4
108	$397,945,911	$395,717,994	$190,614,094	62,827	6,146	10.2

		Short Stay Inpatient by National DRG				
DRG	Total Charges	Covered Charges	Medicare Reimbursement	Total Days	Number of Discharges	Average Total Days
109	$2,809,522,265	$2,795,910,558	$1,244,034,638	468,777	60,946	7.7
110	$2,537,353,673	$2,521,019,779	$1,177,464,478	492,660	53,361	9.2
111	$236,739,443	$235,159,185	$91,896,259	40,757	8,592	4.7
112	$1,209,740,738	$1,202,689,520	$528,720,304	206,701	56,250	3.7
113	$1,329,615,510	$1,311,472,651	$564,633,999	523,557	42,710	12.3
114	$163,959,448	$161,841,081	$69,609,165	74,749	8,828	8.5
115	$562,329,294	$558,647,715	$249,898,488	117,820	14,491	8.1
116	$8,858,553,926	$8,813,949,623	$3,850,745,208	1,204,995	334,384	3.6
117	$58,966,136	$58,326,374	$24,743,218	15,853	3,765	4.2
118	$132,180,797	$131,621,375	$55,508,802	20,802	7,748	2.7
119	$20,807,940	$20,635,864	$8,051,529	6,480	1,324	4.9
120	$896,019,425	$881,543,672	$398,734,136	297,596	36,524	8.1
121	$2,833,536,480	$2,818,336,903	$1,157,996,778	1,044,815	163,538	6.4
122	$904,701,523	$898,170,468	$340,675,846	295,845	79,961	3.7
123	$714,246,018	$710,805,348	$302,529,281	188,500	41,078	4.6
124	$2,159,124,048	$2,142,896,156	$852,216,495	583,177	134,209	4.3
125	$978,096,938	$971,554,273	$359,448,567	224,481	81,147	2.8
126	$158,372,951	$155,936,889	$68,617,488	61,628	5,245	11.7
127	$7,690,712,348	$7,631,543,329	$3,122,011,666	3,615,882	685,026	5.3
128	$76,597,737	$76,005,787	$29,250,374	53,616	9,554	5.6
129	$50,075,392	$49,403,342	$20,865,790	11,558	4,198	2.8
130	$942,176,383	$934,192,903	$383,283,001	504,905	88,436	5.7
131	$180,632,671	$179,314,044	$66,651,700	116,962	27,563	4.2
132	$1,092,246,237	$1,082,327,204	$400,759,451	451,186	149,428	3.0
133	$58,982,569	$58,446,481	$20,946,267	21,695	8,585	2.5
134	$242,809,338	$240,497,420	$82,099,818	119,414	36,614	3.3
135	$78,081,061	$77,357,604	$30,321,760	33,792	7,387	4.6
136	$8,393,726	$8,354,802	$3,051,962	3,415	1,243	2.7
137	$0	$0	$0	0	0	0.0
138	$1,815,909,499	$1,804,471,454	$684,206,221	784,888	196,316	4.0
139	$478,087,111	$474,818,635	$154,364,367	208,312	83,102	2.5
140	$412,603,823	$409,280,649	$145,673,658	187,347	70,572	2.7
141	$764,250,380	$759,317,365	$274,811,335	335,644	91,425	3.7
142	$295,864,684	$293,810,491	$97,515,917	122,042	46,076	2.6
143	$1,254,564,700	$1,243,335,444	$414,814,852	439,211	206,493	2.1
144	$1,136,467,170	$1,118,842,287	$473,277,649	444,114	83,186	5.3
145	$50,966,993	$50,435,867	$19,802,890	20,088	7,313	2.7
146	$339,478,680	$337,466,825	$151,320,799	112,312	10,895	10.3
147	$48,584,075	$48,242,879	$19,678,427	17,173	2,672	6.4
148	$5,051,406,994	$5,018,595,215	$2,337,925,942	1,595,868	130,773	12.2
149	$321,056,645	$319,261,751	$129,468,358	121,980	18,722	6.5
150	$640,522,344	$635,333,710	$281,900,097	226,100	20,029	11.3

	Short Stay Inpatient by National DRG					
DRG	Total Charges	Covered Charges	Medicare Reimbursement	Total Days	Number of Discharges	Average Total Days
151	$72,101,216	$71,555,895	$28,164,413	28,457	4,892	5.8
152	$97,128,915	$96,233,128	$42,912,767	36,272	4,451	8.1
153	$28,793,203	$28,573,270	$11,665,965	11,467	2,136	5.4
154	$1,384,395,424	$1,374,659,277	$659,713,434	385,061	29,183	13.2
155	$103,254,884	$102,508,096	$41,104,984	28,253	6,693	4.2
156						
157	$112,153,924	$110,932,101	$46,015,803	43,307	8,041	5.4
158	$34,078,193	$33,797,172	$11,538,058	11,993	4,735	2.5
159	$249,901,501	$248,173,779	$98,707,729	82,720	16,543	5.0
160	$104,314,773	$103,646,386	$35,705,959	31,366	11,781	2.7
161	$142,833,552	$142,117,555	$54,958,987	47,312	11,262	4.2
162	$50,166,684	$49,797,698	$15,888,330	13,923	7,237	1.9
163						
164	$128,890,756	$128,240,485	$53,930,685	41,091	4,876	8.4
165	$29,643,074	$29,455,249	$10,632,539	10,014	2,093	4.8
166	$59,245,903	$58,822,137	$23,570,469	18,048	3,579	5.0
167	$33,082,397	$32,879,672	$11,381,522	8,646	3,331	2.6
168	$21,669,073	$21,457,353	$8,643,424	6,653	1,399	4.8
169	$7,974,384	$7,891,721	$3,042,672	2,063	881	2.3
170	$378,414,457	$372,291,274	$173,440,038	125,130	11,191	11.2
171	$17,637,456	$17,537,365	$7,366,413	6,058	1,304	4.6
172	$489,257,723	$486,164,446	$205,754,426	216,905	31,155	7.0
173	$22,922,377	$22,723,039	$8,915,637	10,277	2,774	3.7
174	$2,695,076,114	$2,676,533,484	$1,065,702,109	1,165,561	242,866	4.8
175	$202,211,203	$200,676,678	$66,071,116	95,392	32,514	2.9
176	$185,845,253	$184,224,639	$76,385,615	79,949	15,266	5.2
177	$91,615,927	$90,942,273	$33,756,276	42,128	9,296	4.5
178	$26,309,890	$26,197,151	$8,881,630	11,188	3,638	3.1
179	$150,853,985	$149,041,418	$61,648,460	74,504	12,446	6.0
180	$910,069,684	$901,766,293	$353,672,187	464,962	86,641	5.4
181	$156,712,736	$155,554,561	$51,798,177	90,570	26,518	3.4
182	$2,153,165,152	$2,134,375,370	$805,050,536	1,071,054	246,678	4.3
183	$527,328,558	$523,370,539	$175,844,781	247,300	84,767	2.9
184	$509,904	$506,169	$233,198	244	84	2.9
185	$48,789,881	$48,272,814	$19,184,853	22,178	4,886	4.5
186						
187	$6,673,541	$6,457,090	$2,420,946	2,749	700	3.9
188	$973,038,581	$962,146,023	$404,835,006	427,163	76,541	5.6
189	$81,858,088	$81,055,374	$28,917,528	38,112	12,122	3.1
190	$988,448	$956,778	$446,015	381	58	6.6
191	$496,504,667	$490,964,631	$244,384,366	127,078	9,217	13.8
192	$27,661,858	$27,499,630	$11,836,527	7,775	1,180	6.6

			Short Stay Inpatient by National DRG			
DRG	**Total Charges**	**Covered Charges**	**Medicare Reimbursement**	**Total Days**	**Number of Discharges**	**Average Total Days**
193	$209,146,930	$207,831,240	$97,025,260	66,747	5,344	12.5
194	$14,317,676	$14,156,182	$5,691,377	4,928	725	6.8
195	$146,596,754	$146,051,940	$62,240,635	44,382	4,366	10.2
196	$20,598,170	$20,520,897	$8,145,900	6,701	1,170	5.7
197	$531,359,145	$528,215,298	$225,264,171	169,385	18,956	8.9
198	$78,457,611	$77,947,390	$29,570,239	26,446	5,819	4.5
199	$49,915,709	$49,553,974	$22,656,652	17,193	1,809	9.5
200	$37,738,148	$37,377,794	$19,066,168	11,250	1,092	10.3
201	$60,963,136	$60,137,829	$29,522,722	19,525	1,431	13.6
202	$404,210,855	$399,505,165	$176,015,720	168,399	26,277	6.4
203	$455,352,238	$451,910,992	$190,701,121	197,196	29,714	6.6
204	$776,326,900	$766,424,640	$328,082,105	336,833	58,008	5.8
205	$326,166,203	$322,302,477	$138,745,078	143,968	23,275	6.2
206	$16,835,161	$16,611,943	$6,150,004	7,760	1,990	3.9
207	$389,661,299	$387,094,313	$154,724,656	159,224	31,294	5.1
208	$74,571,522	$74,213,959	$25,993,412	29,611	10,198	2.9
209	$7,865,979,388	$7,829,482,367	$3,205,098,840	1,760,253	346,360	5.1
210	$2,453,138,854	$2,441,602,977	$986,213,215	834,905	122,362	6.8
211	$451,207,541	$448,912,370	$169,533,635	157,350	31,855	4.9
212						
213	$203,053,394	$200,365,501	$84,358,062	83,987	9,307	9.0
214	$0	$0	$0	0	0	0.0
215	$0	$0	$0	0	0	0.0
216	$155,366,500	$154,283,797	$66,903,982	58,736	6,056	9.7
217	$599,957,786	$590,117,328	$271,219,466	222,535	16,705	13.3
218	$385,391,415	$382,054,091	$146,986,195	118,645	21,782	5.4
219	$228,000,700	$226,379,908	$80,983,593	64,091	19,833	3.2
220						
221	$0	$0	$0	0	0	0.0
222	$0	$0	$0	0	0	0.0
223	$151,338,261	$150,243,112	$51,397,277	38,632	13,482	2.9
224	$99,389,105	$98,789,388	$33,992,811	21,930	11,321	1.9
225	$73,281,243	$72,702,518	$27,017,635	28,349	5,841	4.9
226	$99,268,286	$98,361,523	$40,506,060	35,929	5,414	6.6
227	$46,355,570	$46,046,816	$16,498,303	13,214	4,844	2.7
228	$29,898,682	$29,718,422	$11,021,700	9,075	2,382	3.8
229	$9,713,759	$9,644,581	$3,408,740	2,792	1,133	2.5
230	$33,572,073	$33,307,762	$12,821,285	11,543	2,216	5.2
231	$190,675,413	$188,829,502	$75,896,791	57,181	11,549	5.0
232	$9,215,956	$9,198,046	$4,190,982	2,348	817	2.9
233	$125,661,199	$124,319,238	$54,756,302	39,182	5,204	7.5
234	$47,539,139	$47,181,945	$18,305,799	11,130	3,222	3.5

		Short Stay Inpatient by National DRG				
DRG	Total Charges	Covered Charges	Medicare Reimbursement	Total Days	Number of Discharges	Average Total Days
235	$48,121,833	$47,237,530	$18,456,633	30,437	5,319	5.7
236	$336,950,674	$333,995,828	$124,590,226	210,259	40,404	5.2
237	$10,556,342	$10,439,244	$3,715,496	6,090	1,716	3.5
238	$127,741,828	$125,769,923	$51,365,261	70,146	8,116	8.6
239	$562,997,851	$558,802,584	$221,624,465	313,156	50,066	6.3
240	$180,786,378	$179,214,831	$75,036,389	77,993	11,596	6.7
241	$24,587,825	$24,214,230	$8,455,787	12,665	3,196	4.0
242	$30,621,408	$30,245,191	$11,752,543	16,696	2,480	6.7
243	$732,989,544	$724,700,513	$261,357,514	423,435	89,448	4.7
244	$120,264,626	$119,071,735	$47,471,506	71,712	13,481	5.3
245	$42,221,460	$41,863,071	$17,031,477	29,116	6,366	4.6
246	$10,820,331	$10,675,571	$4,009,000	6,728	1,522	4.4
247	$122,296,922	$121,194,616	$44,277,072	66,677	17,849	3.7
248	$122,474,998	$121,686,833	$44,730,491	65,754	11,588	5.7
249	$92,393,028	$91,404,377	$35,625,512	44,336	11,671	3.8
250	$28,216,825	$28,014,535	$10,062,870	14,646	3,535	4.1
251	$13,537,338	$13,408,849	$4,160,747	7,334	2,468	3.0
252	$0	$0	$0	0	0	0.0
253	$172,606,546	$170,489,403	$62,391,796	98,299	20,254	4.9
254	$54,626,918	$54,093,885	$16,892,131	35,310	10,696	3.3
255						
256	$62,071,951	$61,301,088	$23,737,700	34,107	6,307	5.4
257	$167,730,428	$166,945,171	$61,823,966	45,521	16,652	2.7
258	$129,472,231	$128,767,062	$44,026,113	31,466	16,260	1.9
259	$43,325,028	$43,078,466	$16,432,632	10,395	3,868	2.7
260	$38,040,020	$37,771,077	$12,271,467	7,051	4,977	1.4
261	$21,664,322	$21,003,531	$7,207,398	4,406	1,909	2.3
262	$6,088,840	$6,070,490	$2,229,209	2,485	627	4.0
263	$573,108,582	$562,066,557	$236,781,938	278,258	23,737	11.7
264	$53,235,650	$52,374,459	$20,013,347	28,675	4,092	7.0
265	$76,505,732	$75,754,312	$33,087,470	26,280	3,883	6.8
266	$29,174,225	$28,904,835	$10,581,023	8,895	2,766	3.2
267	$2,592,602	$2,574,134	$1,048,942	981	234	4.2
268	$14,031,225	$13,599,202	$5,425,399	3,296	929	3.5
269	$172,812,847	$170,042,790	$72,707,729	73,269	8,936	8.2
270	$25,237,000	$25,027,541	$8,716,410	9,335	2,711	3.4
271	$244,197,247	$239,874,488	$94,406,289	150,653	20,766	7.3
272	$66,539,262	$65,770,578	$27,492,797	34,250	5,549	6.2
273	$8,524,534	$8,416,720	$3,229,855	5,258	1,307	4.0
274	$31,511,813	$31,258,939	$12,942,870	15,645	2,377	6.6
275	$2,140,005	$2,114,464	$829,535	1,149	260	4.4
276	$9,693,134	$9,539,262	$3,483,569	5,750	1,206	4.8

	Short Stay Inpatient by National DRG					
DRG	Total Charges	Covered Charges	Medicare Reimbursement	Total Days	Number of Discharges	Average Total Days
277	$869,193,898	$859,459,183	$327,456,899	512,571	89,426	5.7
278	$192,413,769	$190,631,627	$65,734,295	133,162	30,873	4.3
279						
280	$126,515,049	$124,598,231	$43,622,922	67,446	15,989	4.2
281	$39,384,071	$38,862,742	$11,641,552	21,918	7,294	3.0
282						
283	$48,198,060	$47,454,702	$19,101,343	26,556	5,759	4.6
284	$9,509,055	$9,353,406	$3,198,813	5,885	1,880	3.1
285	$148,310,153	$146,096,356	$64,558,813	64,997	6,310	10.3
286	$57,832,933	$57,610,854	$26,303,229	13,526	2,113	6.4
287	$128,494,556	$126,491,352	$56,109,590	60,902	5,786	10.5
288	$73,430,352	$72,407,236	$29,605,514	15,410	2,710	5.7
289	$57,550,428	$57,148,653	$22,209,649	14,626	4,843	3.0
290	$95,605,982	$95,158,021	$35,865,652	20,823	8,971	2.3
291	$548,368	$546,239	$217,345	123	67	1.8
292	$155,740,837	$152,460,618	$67,907,362	51,970	5,083	10.2
293	$6,005,734	$5,964,649	$2,301,705	2,086	390	5.3
294	$778,278,850	$769,208,091	$298,682,749	411,406	88,951	4.6
295	$31,705,641	$30,613,954	$11,830,031	13,641	3,609	3.8
296	$2,326,731,757	$2,305,734,749	$927,936,194	1,247,662	241,497	5.2
297	$254,401,325	$252,142,807	$88,566,142	150,612	44,161	3.4
298	$629,652	$624,526	$295,685	303	103	2.9
299	$12,510,866	$11,968,124	$4,950,479	6,449	1,210	5.3
300	$204,628,541	$203,017,592	$83,781,380	99,757	16,248	6.1
301	$23,403,211	$23,217,268	$8,288,812	11,862	3,263	3.6
302	$687,026,911	$669,163,722	$191,249,535	76,465	8,420	9.1
303	$574,511,917	$571,574,174	$265,397,956	168,530	19,991	8.4
304	$344,563,033	$339,829,873	$157,537,564	105,338	12,037	8.8
305	$42,357,980	$42,087,397	$16,857,236	11,131	3,047	3.7
306	$105,745,544	$105,152,278	$42,377,518	41,678	7,405	5.6
307	$14,839,474	$14,764,686	$5,252,070	4,787	2,117	2.3
308	$142,864,265	$141,373,759	$60,796,462	46,912	7,562	6.2
309	$44,078,157	$43,765,398	$16,317,155	9,548	4,145	2.3
310	$309,689,185	$308,046,083	$119,389,384	106,432	24,186	4.4
311	$55,725,319	$55,371,576	$18,788,943	14,839	8,096	1.8
312	$19,106,573	$18,767,047	$7,345,468	6,763	1,507	4.5
313	$4,994,962	$4,972,123	$1,778,056	1,394	601	2.3
314						
315	$720,829,385	$708,894,688	$329,673,601	212,403	30,288	7.0
316	$1,623,126,409	$1,603,877,295	$702,233,381	703,690	106,101	6.6
317	$11,534,785	$11,312,491	$4,955,823	4,426	1,543	2.9
318	$75,666,154	$75,087,255	$31,327,787	34,663	5,727	6.1

		Short Stay Inpatient by National DRG				
DRG	**Total Charges**	**Covered Charges**	**Medicare Reimbursement**	**Total Days**	**Number of Discharges**	**Average Total Days**
319	$3,480,981	$3,458,708	$1,392,131	1,311	466	2.8
320	$1,827,738,580	$1,810,637,050	$713,417,319	1,005,861	188,954	5.3
321	$192,369,504	$190,756,386	$67,532,887	116,108	30,558	3.8
322	$511,216	$497,989	$189,188	263	65	4.0
323	$158,300,846	$157,244,724	$55,597,376	56,550	17,509	3.2
324	$37,497,510	$37,197,440	$10,642,032	14,296	7,590	1.9
325	$60,802,663	$60,253,334	$23,053,096	31,927	8,316	3.8
326	$13,851,817	$13,716,031	$4,732,409	7,367	2,740	2.7
327	$60,175	$60,175	$25,208	34	11	3.1
328	$5,676,308	$5,652,307	$2,050,332	2,466	674	3.7
329	$462,235	$461,762	$175,800	171	79	2.2
330	$0	$0	$0	0	0	0.0
331	$572,662,099	$564,874,146	$232,177,102	260,841	46,924	5.6
332	$36,827,081	$36,457,223	$13,522,247	16,626	5,007	3.3
333	$4,014,549	$3,846,708	$1,637,234	1,619	323	5.0
334	$188,076,271	$186,977,466	$74,840,462	51,713	10,635	4.9
335	$157,576,089	$156,412,349	$59,435,891	40,074	12,129	3.3
336	$373,035,435	$370,797,524	$142,664,545	132,283	37,846	3.5
337	$205,831,584	$204,707,924	$70,234,696	64,631	30,501	2.1
338	$16,680,110	$16,576,542	$6,492,126	6,339	1,242	5.1
339	$20,714,286	$20,661,996	$8,038,804	7,512	1,636	4.6
340						
341	$52,059,112	$51,493,132	$19,655,846	11,525	3,793	3.0
342	$5,992,071	$5,945,590	$2,361,817	2,209	679	3.3
343	$0	$0	$0	0	0	0.0
344	$51,555,156	$51,241,577	$18,841,769	8,424	3,557	2.4
345	$13,634,908	$13,518,406	$5,264,501	4,933	1,287	3.8
346	$52,621,305	$52,027,669	$20,219,679	27,165	4,558	6.0
347	$3,104,244	$3,063,088	$1,151,469	1,235	394	3.1
348	$25,006,674	$24,813,029	$9,416,411	12,938	3,097	4.2
349	$3,154,137	$3,134,773	$1,057,813	1,639	636	2.6
350	$50,992,628	$50,289,889	$17,979,035	27,974	6,357	4.4
351	$0	$0	$0	0	0	0.0
352	$6,167,009	$6,116,972	$2,362,752	3,063	774	4.0
353	$60,708,113	$60,065,261	$28,703,765	16,815	2,594	6.5
354	$142,095,163	$141,534,665	$59,166,349	45,206	7,725	5.9
355	$60,603,453	$60,245,137	$22,349,508	18,335	5,576	3.3
356	$213,813,160	$212,794,854	$74,749,529	58,165	25,379	2.3
357	$157,858,870	$157,240,239	$71,522,331	48,076	5,674	8.5
358	$282,221,324	$280,188,431	$110,912,748	88,992	20,623	4.3
359	$282,011,956	$280,513,158	$99,179,187	82,624	30,275	2.7
360	$160,197,584	$159,360,512	$58,272,210	46,017	16,102	2.9

	Short Stay Inpatient by National DRG					
DRG	Total Charges	Covered Charges	Medicare Reimbursement	Total Days	Number of Discharges	Average Total Days
361	$5,058,519	$5,016,244	$2,045,409	1,156	388	3.0
362						
363	$29,320,396	$29,102,013	$11,136,420	10,198	2,942	3.5
364	$16,004,596	$15,881,823	$5,730,383	6,458	1,679	3.8
365	$38,348,020	$38,227,717	$16,603,017	12,624	1,745	7.2
366	$63,891,135	$63,446,334	$28,218,883	30,520	4,526	6.7
367	$4,184,770	$4,132,838	$1,577,864	1,893	600	3.2
368	$41,132,919	$40,790,612	$16,243,954	20,338	3,148	6.5
369	$21,091,775	$20,824,998	$7,420,154	10,573	3,223	3.3
370	$16,368,233	$16,008,053	$6,838,269	7,012	1,176	6.0
371	$11,507,700	$11,287,773	$4,079,790	5,065	1,396	3.6
372	$7,140,424	$7,043,611	$2,655,842	3,179	970	3.3
373	$18,920,775	$18,596,130	$5,616,489	8,996	3,999	2.2
374	$1,059,341	$921,004	$344,636	398	130	3.1
375	$78,231	$75,758	$26,883	25	11	2.3
376	$2,028,972	$1,976,974	$840,014	1,219	294	4.1
377	$1,430,429	$1,420,205	$513,840	374	52	7.2
378	$1,652,185	$1,635,039	$694,607	391	162	2.4
379	$1,950,379	$1,913,107	$656,812	1,187	344	3.5
380	$349,430	$276,473	$62,762	129	62	2.1
381	$1,445,894	$1,432,494	$538,228	388	156	2.5
382	$122,005	$121,921	$31,270	59	46	1.3
383	$12,790,163	$12,486,746	$5,056,713	7,737	1,911	4.0
384	$540,877	$534,890	$169,743	260	121	2.1
385						
386	$0	$0	$0	0	0	0.0
387	$0	$0	$0	0	0	0.0
388	$0	$0	$0	0	0	0.0
389	$1,239,011	$1,226,531	$420,592	338	18	18.8
390	$254,584	$254,584	$83,554	51	14	3.6
391						
392	$88,576,285	$87,639,378	$40,422,147	23,041	2,375	9.7
393	$0	$0	$0	0	0	0.0
394	$40,185,956	$39,600,407	$17,654,973	13,617	1,907	7.1
395	$821,481,296	$784,771,971	$316,814,247	388,981	88,218	4.4
396	$207,046	$207,046	$103,057	73	16	4.6
397	$271,319,133	$268,820,094	$120,542,310	92,428	17,811	5.2
398	$270,365,270	$267,999,078	$114,216,841	108,105	18,117	6.0
399	$13,517,869	$13,434,074	$5,297,755	6,331	1,753	3.6
400	$213,080,452	$211,744,754	$100,612,429	61,567	6,752	9.1
401	$185,460,031	$184,309,874	$82,508,590	64,193	5,698	11.3
402	$20,522,590	$20,334,638	$7,297,724	6,239	1,531	4.1

			Short Stay Inpatient by National DRG			
DRG	Total Charges	Covered Charges	Medicare Reimbursement	Total Days	Number of Discharges	Average Total Days
403	$669,944,653	$663,578,222	$299,317,408	266,139	32,915	8.1
404	$48,919,413	$48,546,481	$19,665,605	20,632	4,821	4.3
405	$0	$0	$0	0	0	0.0
406	$88,743,943	$88,032,022	$40,437,191	26,233	2,615	10.0
407	$11,726,122	$11,683,149	$4,694,828	3,427	755	4.5
408	$57,401,064	$56,994,647	$26,548,234	18,334	2,277	8.1
409	$40,974,751	$40,670,716	$17,445,585	17,108	2,882	5.9
410	$433,138,778	$429,791,665	$178,009,371	138,812	35,331	3.9
411	$80,558	$76,800	$30,335	32	14	2.3
412	$217,463	$215,661	$41,588	72	30	2.4
413	$94,019,684	$93,013,806	$41,444,309	44,185	6,180	7.1
414	$6,842,767	$6,783,044	$2,877,176	3,487	784	4.4
415	$1,684,418,190	$1,649,932,419	$790,758,569	565,544	39,319	14.4
416	$3,284,222,590	$3,242,565,495	$1,349,448,944	1,373,773	185,469	7.4
417	$315,712	$315,529	$101,183	114	23	5.0
418	$279,289,399	$276,501,918	$118,371,385	142,559	23,238	6.1
419	$153,736,832	$152,171,152	$63,394,352	73,880	15,628	4.7
420	$21,875,391	$21,762,897	$7,786,539	10,928	3,133	3.5
421	$88,325,909	$87,586,506	$31,621,823	44,139	11,598	3.8
422	$617,983	$608,226	$258,741	256	85	3.0
423	$156,515,830	$153,228,750	$65,759,268	62,021	7,611	8.1
424	$76,126,048	$73,522,980	$31,198,063	44,917	2,694	16.7
425	$168,569,804	$166,311,040	$68,011,907	102,845	20,506	5.0
426	$146,264,683	$143,136,984	$62,815,255	122,239	17,808	6.9
427	$46,379,766	$45,711,589	$21,180,735	40,921	6,376	6.4
428	$34,781,613	$33,487,981	$14,994,021	30,873	3,365	9.2
429	$793,231,921	$783,013,028	$373,257,892	650,383	65,097	10.0
430	$4,038,846,883	$3,923,529,089	$1,790,710,096	3,502,691	314,054	11.2
431	$16,045,286	$15,607,138	$7,613,390	14,189	1,494	9.5
432	$5,967,043	$5,703,189	$2,499,448	4,108	641	6.4
433	$24,960,491	$24,066,920	$9,064,233	20,067	6,418	3.1
434	$245,405,983	$241,237,764	$101,401,440	154,376	28,385	5.4
435	$120,206,427	$116,716,781	$49,617,887	101,034	21,316	4.7
436	$29,810,558	$29,138,563	$12,935,114	42,420	3,324	12.8
437	$78,590,130	$77,507,991	$33,840,931	90,022	10,373	8.7
438	$0	$0	$0	0	0	0.0
439	$31,723,036	$31,184,588	$13,804,688	11,586	1,375	8.4
440	$121,120,537	$119,038,056	$56,363,654	47,408	5,240	9.0
441	$6,943,757	$6,845,335	$2,421,604	1,960	607	3.2
442	$441,514,697	$435,092,844	$195,763,844	133,506	15,723	8.5
443	$43,914,213	$43,379,414	$16,395,727	13,044	3,780	3.5
444	$45,648,249	$44,916,106	$15,889,316	22,825	5,394	4.2

		Short Stay Inpatient by National DRG				
DRG	**Total Charges**	**Covered Charges**	**Medicare Reimbursement**	**Total Days**	**Number of Discharges**	**Average Total Days**
445	$15,154,496	$14,774,242	$4,703,280	8,018	2,543	3.2
446	$0	$0	$0	0	0	0.0
447	$32,074,328	$31,736,726	$11,550,739	13,649	5,524	2.5
448	$0	$0	$0	0	0	0.0
449	$282,270,268	$278,893,045	$111,756,007	110,472	29,081	3.8
450	$35,112,881	$34,585,356	$11,430,636	14,747	7,147	2.1
451						
452	$273,047,615	$269,524,192	$117,594,233	113,144	23,200	4.9
453	$30,557,237	$30,344,448	$11,307,579	14,444	5,123	2.8
454	$41,910,743	$41,576,224	$16,040,525	18,515	4,030	4.6
455	$5,681,439	$5,449,650	$1,754,251	2,488	958	2.6
456	$0	$0	$0	0	0	0.0
457	$0	$0	$0	0	0	0.0
458	$0	$0	$0	0	0	0.0
459	$0	$0	$0	0	0	0.0
460	$0	$0	$0	0	0	0.0
461	$217,352,662	$214,614,743	$86,984,420	104,834	8,037	13.0
462	$4,943,500,960	$4,905,059,723	$2,527,143,800	3,461,455	265,937	13.0
463	$188,383,230	$186,513,101	$72,054,366	105,166	23,187	4.5
464	$38,594,924	$38,340,439	$13,604,472	22,908	6,829	3.4
465	$2,008,481	$1,988,452	$953,943	956	277	3.5
466	$25,199,640	$24,649,995	$11,331,886	12,295	2,159	5.7
467	$7,500,562	$7,144,974	$2,995,102	4,434	1,273	3.5
468	$2,554,253,942	$2,513,561,936	$1,178,510,234	783,604	60,243	13.0
469	$0	$0	$0	0	0	0.0
470						
471	$403,512,237	$401,603,956	$174,515,528	65,284	11,753	5.6
472	$0	$0	$0	0	0	0.0
473	$330,671,098	$328,815,231	$176,526,294	100,020	7,843	12.8
474	$0	$0	$0	0	0	0.0
475	$4,605,895,272	$4,534,641,668	$2,120,340,989	1,215,922	108,221	11.2
476	$103,125,721	$102,693,418	$46,544,127	45,391	4,168	10.9
477	$542,462,824	$534,849,844	$228,593,014	208,721	25,574	8.2
478	$2,981,385,107	$2,957,303,918	$1,331,303,493	798,010	109,246	7.3
479	$390,586,328	$388,709,730	$157,195,354	83,543	24,179	3.5
480	$124,050,021	$120,667,664	$54,829,753	13,682	683	20.0
481	$55,263,517	$50,979,753	$25,106,202	11,838	482	24.6
482	$278,760,643	$276,640,597	$134,114,809	77,671	5,989	13.0
483	$8,225,980,827	$8,058,975,555	$3,904,512,297	1,710,213	43,172	39.6
484	$20,921,108	$20,218,287	$9,479,673	4,308	333	12.9
485	$111,264,505	$109,624,167	$48,347,514	29,216	2,995	9.8
486	$131,020,048	$127,847,889	$54,043,332	25,862	2,079	12.4

		Short Stay Inpatient by National DRG				
DRG	Total Charges	Covered Charges	Medicare Reimbursement	Total Days	Number of Discharges	Average Total Days
487	$83,145,204	$82,224,481	$33,113,961	27,669	3,655	7.6
488	$51,666,330	$50,985,956	$25,759,714	13,797	798	17.3
489	$357,439,251	$351,403,220	$172,688,042	121,248	14,327	8.5
490	$77,105,384	$75,775,529	$32,246,387	30,313	5,561	5.5
491	$231,518,008	$230,139,991	$90,325,234	42,556	12,324	3.5
492	$149,870,884	$149,207,069	$81,184,104	45,078	2,886	15.6
493	$1,085,007,445	$1,078,902,735	$450,138,862	319,000	55,430	5.8
494	$328,277,202	$326,494,892	$120,647,559	73,776	30,193	2.4
495	$31,475,553	$30,477,156	$12,119,373	3,135	197	15.9
496	$104,941,597	$104,305,889	$45,871,631	14,521	1,486	9.8
497	$844,062,501	$838,564,269	$339,575,629	149,325	24,105	6.2
498	$508,025,978	$504,337,489	$178,609,356	74,920	22,538	3.3
499	$510,259,042	$507,211,307	$203,207,272	144,304	30,657	4.7
500	$489,562,144	$486,487,606	$177,338,825	116,098	44,476	2.6
501	$68,918,728	$67,593,225	$29,405,212	24,172	2,205	11.0
502	$10,289,194	$10,150,862	$4,158,653	3,824	585	6.5
503	$79,683,766	$79,021,340	$29,912,997	22,661	5,663	4.0
504	$24,557,075	$24,453,620	$12,020,537	3,902	132	29.6
505	$4,666,484	$4,651,876	$2,290,237	661	165	4.0
506	$68,730,518	$68,284,666	$32,073,201	17,979	1,032	17.4
507	$8,200,700	$8,134,953	$3,783,763	2,776	322	8.6
508	$12,187,537	$12,058,142	$6,136,524	5,540	705	7.9
509	$1,749,123	$1,681,108	$703,447	878	192	4.6
510	$32,408,353	$32,094,480	$14,397,457	12,821	1,714	7.5
511	$7,112,365	$7,042,701	$3,138,810	3,185	636	5.0
TOTAL LINE	$193,110,452,056	$191,220,306,253	$81,288,767,430	70,987,303	11,778,705	6.0

Source: www.hcfa.gov/stats/medpar/medpar.htm

Zero or small cells suppress to conform to privacy guidelines, therefore, sum of column will not equal the total.

AHIMA Certification:
Your Valuable Career Asset

AHIMA offers a variety of credentials whether you're just starting out in the health information management (HIM) field, are an advanced coding professional, or play an important privacy or security role at your facility. Employers are looking for your commitment to the field and a certain competency level. AHIMA credentials help you stand out from the crowd of resumés.

✔ Registered Health Information Administrator/Registered Health Information Technician

✔ Certified Coding Associate (entry-level)

✔ Certified Coding Specialist (advanced)

✔ Certified Coding Specialist—Physician-based (advanced)

✔ Certified in Healthcare Privacy

✔ Certified in Healthcare Security (offered by HIMSS through AHIMA)

✔ Certified in Healthcare Privacy and Security (AHIMA in conjunction with HIMSS)

In recent AHIMA-sponsored research groups, healthcare executives and recruiters cited three reasons for preferring credentialed personnel:

1. Assurance of current knowledge through continued education
2. Possession of field-tested experience
3. Verification of base level competency

AHIMA is a premier organization for HIM professionals, with more than 41,000 members nationwide. AHIMA certification carries a strong reputation for quality—the requirements for our certification are rigorous.

AHIMA exams are computer-based and available throughout the year.

Make the right move...pair your degree and experience with AHIMA certification to maximize your career possibilities.

For more information on AHIMA credentials and how to sit for the exams, you can either visit our Web site at **www.ahima.org/certification**, send an e-mail to **certdept@ahima.org**, or call **(800) 335-5535**.

Look for These Quality AHIMA Publications at Bookstores, Libraries, and Online

Applying Inpatient Coding Skills under Prospective Payment

Basic CPT/HCPCS Coding

Basic Healthcare Statistics for Health Information Management Professionals

Basic ICD-9-CM Coding

Coding and Reimbursement under the Outpatient Prospective Payment System

Coding in Context

CPT/HCPCS Coding and Reimbursement for Physician Services

Documentation and Reimbursement for Home Care and Hospice Programs

Documentation for Ambulatory Care

Documentation for Acute Care

Effective Management of Coding Services

Finance Principles for the Health Information Manager

Health Information Management: Concepts, Principles, and Practice

Health Information Management Compliance: A Model Program for Healthcare Organizations

Health Information Management Technology

ICD-9-CM Diagnostic Coding and Reimbursement for Physician Services

Performance Improvement in Healthcare: A Tool for Programmed Learning

Reimbursement Methodologies for Healthcare Services

Need to Know More?

Textbook details and easy ordering are available online on the AHIMA Web site at **www.ahima.org.** Click on "Professional Development." In addition to textbooks, AHIMA offers other educational products such as online training programs and audio seminars. For textbook content questions, contact **publications@ahima.org,** and for sales information contact **resources@ahima.org**.

Join AHIMA and Gain "Insider Knowledge"

The Exclusive Province of AHIMA Members!

Nowhere else will you find the kind of "Insider Knowledge" you can acquire from our highly active membership of more than 41,000 health information management (HIM) professionals! Combine this depth of exclusive knowledge with your fresh ideas and new perspectives and you've come up with a winning combination, one that will lead you in new directions in professionalism and career growth.

When you join AHIMA, your most prominent benefit is "Insider Knowledge." All other benefits relate back to the knowledge you gain. Here are just a few areas where "Insider Knowledge" helps you thrive:

Workplace solutions: From columns on HIPAA, coding, and best practices in the award-winning *Journal of AHIMA*, to *Advantage* e-alerts on industry news, to the *Advantage* newsletter, and more, you get the kind of insider knowledge you won't find elsewhere…the kind of knowledge that puts you ahead of the competition

Career growth: From certification to education, AHIMA membership offers you exclusive benefits for making the most of your career, because you have the knowledge to excel and lead

Networking: Where else can you get access to more than 41,000 of your professional peers? Especially with our unique virtual network, Communities of Practice, which gives you the ability to search for and join forces with like-minded professionals to solve problems and strategize to make the most of your career!

Membership in AHIMA is a bargain. Active membership is only $135 per year, and student membership is just $20 per year.

Need more reasons to join? Go to www.ahima.org/membership to see how joining America's premier HIM Association benefits you.

Insider Knowledge…
Join Today and Gain Instant Access!

AHIMA
AMERICAN HEALTH INFORMATION
MANAGEMENT ASSOCIATION®

Sample Audit Tools on Disk

The following sample audit tools are available on the enclosed computer disk, were created using Microsoft Word, and are compatible with Word 97–2000 and 6.0/95–RTF:

Ambulatory coding review worksheet

Coding audit review sheet

Coding audit summary

Coding compliance review: Inpatient summary

Coding compliance review: Outpatient summary

Coding DRG variation form

Coding services review tool

Coding validation worksheet

Compliance audit

Daily worksheet: Inpatient cases

HHPPS coding audit tool (©2002 hiqmConsulting)

Inpatient rebilling log

Inpatient review: Variations by coder

OBQM clinical record review: UTIs (©2002 hiqmConsulting)

OBQM clinical record review: Wounds (©2002 hiqmConsulting)

Outpatient rebilling log

Prebill review form

Rebilling log

Rebilling summary coding change

Rehabilitation functional independence measure (©2002 Patricia Trela and Anna Tran)

Rehabilitation patient assessment instrument (©2002 Patricia Trela and Anna Tran)

SNF PPS compliance audit: Medicare Part A

Statistics for coding quality monitoring